ADRIFT

A TRUE STORY OF SURVIVAL AT SEA

V. Sudarshan works as Executive Editor, *The New Indian Express*. He has been a journalist for over 26 years, and was Foreign Editor of *The Pioneer*, a New Delhi based newspaper and Senior Analyst at *Outlook*, a weekly news magazine where he wrote on foreign affairs. His previous book, *Anatomy of an Abduction: How the Indian Hostages in Iraq Were Freed* was published by Penguin in 2008. It is in the process of being made into a film. His collection of short stories, *A Sense of Ending*, was published by the Calcutta Writers Workshop in 1988. He lives in Chennai.

ADRIFT

A TRUE STORY OF SURVIVAL AT SEA

V. Sudarshan

Maps and Illustrations by
Rudraa Abirami Sudarshan

hachette
INDIA

First published in 2013 by Hachette India
Registered name: Hachette Book Publishing India Pvt. Ltd
An Hachette UK company
www.hachetteindia.com

SRD

ISBN 978-93-5009-629-1

Hachette Book Publishing India Pvt. Ltd
4th/5th Floors, Corporate Centre,
Sector 44, Gurgaon 122003, India

Typeset in Granjon 11.5/14.5
by Ram Das Lal, NCR Delhi

Printed and Bound in India by
Manipal Technologies Limited, Manipal

MIX
Paper from responsible sources
FSC™ C043100

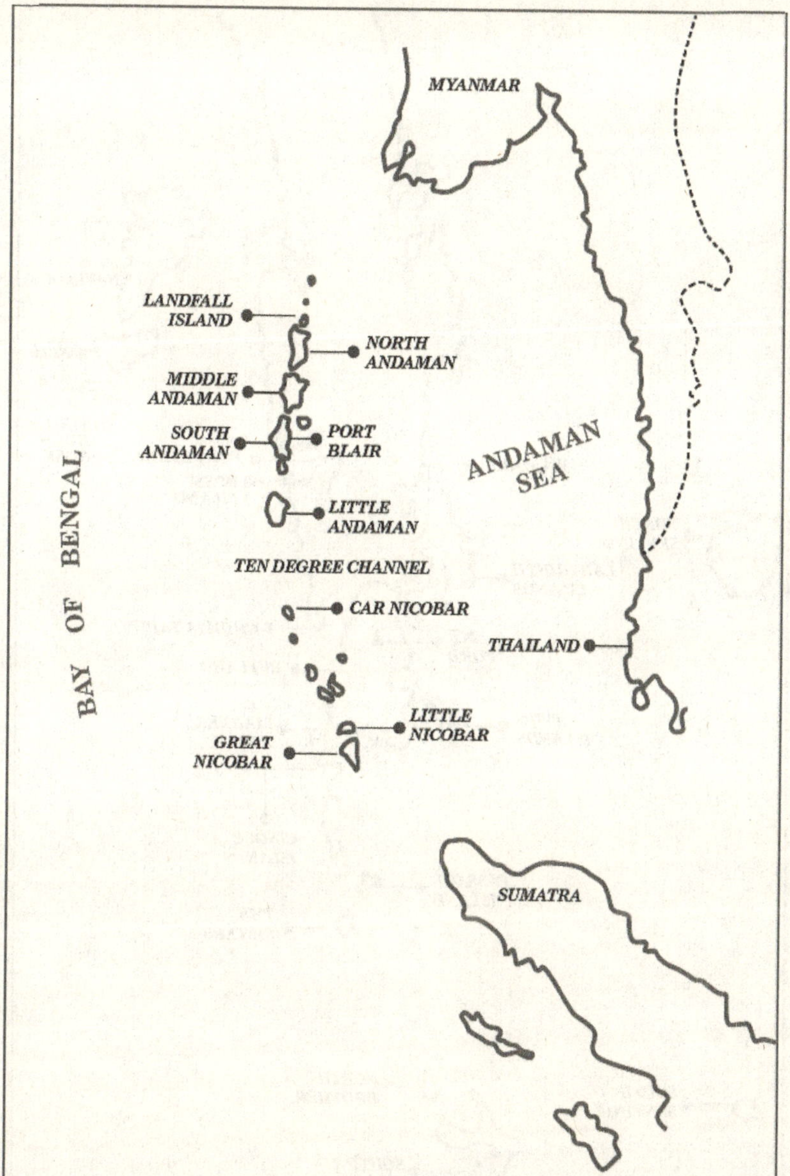
MYANMAR
LANDFALL ISLAND
NORTH ANDAMAN
MIDDLE ANDAMAN
SOUTH ANDAMAN
PORT BLAIR
ANDAMAN SEA
BAY OF BENGAL
LITTLE ANDAMAN
TEN DEGREE CHANNEL
CAR NICOBAR
THAILAND
LITTLE NICOBAR
GREAT NICOBAR
SUMATRA

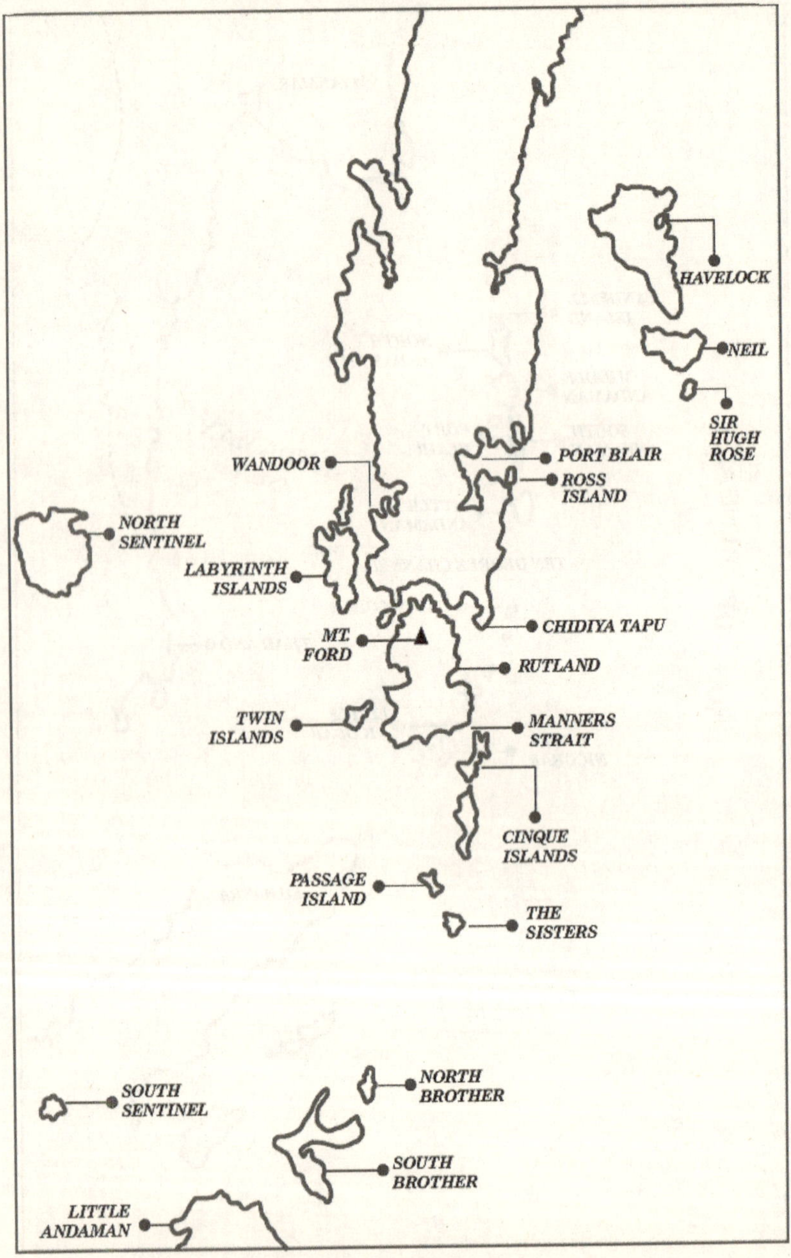
HAVELOCK
NEIL
SIR HUGH ROSE
PORT BLAIR
WANDOOR
ROSS ISLAND
NORTH SENTINEL
LABYRINTH ISLANDS
CHIDIYA TAPU
MT. FORD
RUTLAND
TWIN ISLANDS
MANNERS STRAIT
CINQUE ISLANDS
PASSAGE ISLAND
THE SISTERS
NORTH BROTHER
SOUTH SENTINEL
SOUTH BROTHER
LITTLE ANDAMAN

To Jonia and Dinky

Foreword

I first heard about the adventure of Commander Avtar Singh Baath in the summer of 2007, some years after the events described here had transpired, second hand, in a coffee shop, late one Saturday afternoon in Chennai. Ralphy Simon D'Cruz and his wife Jonia, friends of Commander Baath, narrated the events in about half an hour before they left for the airport to catch a flight back to Port Blair. As I listened transfixed to the story of Commander Baath, Bruno Beauregard, Camille Pascal, Rama Rao Sr, Himanshu Mallik and Rama Rao Jr, my coffee remained untouched and then it became too cold to drink. Maybe it was the way D'Cruz narrated the tale, the way he understated the drama, or maybe it was because it was set in Andaman and Nicobar islands that I felt drawn to it.

I had spent some very impressionable years in those islands trying not to grow up, islands which lay beyond the imagination of most Indians, a series of small specks in maps where the Bay of Bengal was marked, nearer to Myanmar and Thailand than India. I remember the glitter of the Andaman Sea from the verandah of our house which sat low, with sloping asbestos roofing to fend off incessant tropical downpours that continued sometimes for days on end, on a gentle hill behind the Lieutenant Governor's sprawling estate. Beyond the azure sea, far beyond where the eye could see, were islands with British sounding names – Neil Island, Havelock Island, Sir Hugh Rose Island, Rutland Island; from Landfall Island in the north, off Myanmar through Smith Island all the way down to Pygmalion Point (now called Indira Point) in the south, where I have heard it said that should you climb the tallest tree on a clear night the only lights you will see twinkle other than a million stars are the lights from Indonesia.

Of course, I now realise that this couldn't possibly have been true: Indonesia was more than 60 nautical miles away; but during those island years I was convinced that events described in many of the books that I greedily devoured – *Robinson Crusoe*, *Treasure Island*, *Reader's Digest* condensed version of the *Kon Tiki Expedition* and *Lord of the Flies* – could easily have taken place in any one of the hundreds of uninhabited islands in the Andaman and Nicobar archipelago. In some of those islands lived near-naked tribes looking more African than Indian, with flared nostrils, curly hair and very dark skin, tribes which shot arrows, both at fish and at human trespassers. On the floor of the local marine museum near Aberdeen jetty, facing Ross Island, languished an impossibly long whale skeleton, longer than anything I could ever imagine, while a wicked-looking petrified swordfish dominated the entire wall of the enormous room, its tooth longer than the length of both my hands. Those days there was no television, only imagination. These creatures could have leapt right out of *Twenty Thousand Leagues Under the Sea*; there were open shark jaws with crazy teeth that stared at me silently; if someone had told me that this was one of the twenty-nine sharks Hemingway's old man fought off as they attacked the marlin he had wrestled and finally subdued, I would have readily believed it.

For centuries, pirates had roamed the Andaman Sea; the capital was named Port Blair, after a British East India Company surveyor who weighed anchor here, at Chatham Island, in an imperial outreach to fend off pirates and malaria; Chatham once housed Asia's biggest match factory. The islands had seen Danes, the British and the heartless Japanese rule them; in Campbell Bay, where I had tagged along with my father whose job as a veterinarian took him wherever there was livestock and poultry, I had seen the white skeleton of a Japanese Zero, perched precariously on the ledge of a steep hill which fell precipitously down to the rocks where the sea crashed relentlessly.

No one went to the Andamans except those the British condemned to its penal confines to torture, hang or resettle, and later government officials, like my father, who were posted there, and much later tourists subsidized by the government to promote the islands. The flights from Calcutta to Port Blair had a refuelling stop in exotic Rangoon then; I remember the first time we took a Mughal Lines ship, M V Akbar, to Port Blair, it took seven memorable nights of sailing instead of three because a ferry had gone down in muddy Hoogly after our ship left Diamond Harbour in what was then called Calcutta.

So when D'Cruz suggested that I should visit Port Blair to meet Commander Baath I lost no time in planning a holiday there along with my family; my daughter turned nine in Port Blair; there was a new baby whale bone in the naval museum, laid out for visitors, one that had beached in Ross Island and died. Its carcass rotted even while it became a tourist attraction. I subsequently travelled to the Andaman and Nicobar islands several times to get the narrative together. Naturally some of the people I have written about were very reluctant to have their story told; some did not want it to see the light of day, even ten years after the events described here; some of their names I have changed to offer them some privacy. I have also switched the chronology of some of the events, in order to bring about a greater narrative coherence. This book would not have been possible without the exceptional co-operation extended by Commander Baath, his wife Mona, their children, Karan, Aman, Nishanth, and the people who worked with them. I thank the Coast Guard commander in Chennai, Satya Prakash Sharma, the former head of coast guard in Port Blair, S K Dey, for making it easier for this book to acquire this form. For her unstinting support, her valuable comments and suggestions, for going through the drafts and for being there every step of the way, I want to thank my wife, Reeja. I especially want to thank my daughter Rudraa for her patience and skill at drawing the figures that you see in this book and for the maps of the Andaman and Nicobar islands.

PROLOGUE

Crocodile Cove

Radhanagar Beach is one of seven beaches at Havelock Island. It curves in a three kilometre wide arc that lets the sea in. The fine powdery sand is blinding white in the sun and hot under the feet. It hasn't rained for over a week and by three thirty in the afternoon the relentless late April sun has warmed the aquamarine sea. Further out the colour of the sea changes imperceptibly to deep blue. In the distance, out in the open sea, a white motor boat makes its way slowly. There are maybe a dozen people in the water. A couple stands on the first line of breakers where the waves crash. The water comes up to the girl's breasts after the wave passes. When the wave comes at them, she holds his hand and they both jump to stay above the water, shouting in excitement. A young boy in fluorescent -orange swimming trunks throws a yellow tennis ball into the sea and waits for the whooshing waves to bring the ball bobbing back. At the treeline where the beach ends, there is a woman who reads a book, her dark glasses pushed back over her wide forehead. She is blond and her hair is cut close, just below her ears. Strands of hair keep falling over her eyes, and she pushes them back. The treeline is about fifty metres from where the sea gushes gently onto the sand, chasing crabs out of their holes at the waterline. When the sea retreats the sand glistens like glass.

Clumps of seaweed lie strewn, all the way to where the trees begin. The ones that have just been brought in by the sea are a pallid green; those that have been washed up earlier are turning brown. The shrieks of the couple jumping against the waves carry over to the young woman reading the book. Whenever she looks out to the glinting sea where her companion is swimming, she slides her glasses on to her nose, and rests her hardbound book on her lap. Behind her are tall mahua trees that rise thickly toward the sky. Their ash-coloured trunks like giant pillars that support the thick canopy of branches and leaves which block out the sun. In the shade it is cool and dark and reasonably safe from the sandflies. Butterflies hover over the clumps of kewda growing in the shadow of the trees, green leaves rising like writhing snakes from the ground. Hermit crabs scuttle about the sand near the fallen tree trunk she is sitting on. There is a flutter above her head and she looks up at the bird, a blue-black Andaman drongo, settling on a branch. It is smaller than a pigeon and has a tail which forks into two long tapering parts. It looks this way and that and cheeps. She had seen this bird the day before. She takes out a bottle from the bag lying beside her on the sand when she notices a small hermit crab crawling into her bag. She puts the bottle down and gently removes the crab from the bag. It has retreated into its shell. She straightens her palm and places the small crab on it. In a little while the crab emerges from its white shell speckled with red and moves about her palm. It tickles her palm. She can hear her companion calling out to her. She looks up at him, coming out of the sea, removing his snorkelling mask.

I just saw a moray eel, he shouts, probably the same one we saw yesterday. The crab reaches the edge of her palm and falls off onto the sand and retreats into its shell.

He calls out to her and says, Let's get some snorkelling done before the sun goes down.

The girl looks at her watch: it is four. She shrugs her shoulders and closes her book with a snap, picks up her bag, puts the bottle back inside it, and stands up abruptly. She is petite, not more than twenty five. She adjusts a navy blue and white towel around her waist, draws it more tightly around her and puts her book inside the bag and starts walking briskly towards the cove on the far right, beyond a fringe of rocks that rise out of the sea all the way to the tree line about a kilometre to the right of her. Occasionally she pauses to scratch her legs, which are covered with red marks from sand fly bites.

I have a feeling that today we will see something we didn't see yesterday, her companion is saying.

Maybe we will see the moray eel again, she responds. Before the sun goes down, she adds after a pause. He smiles, reaches out for her hand, and clasps it.

How is the book going? he asks. Scary?

Not really. It's only a book, she responds.

Yes, but I read somewhere it is based on a real-life incident. And right now, it is situation-inappropriate, he says, without looking at her.

She looks at him and says, Well I'm not getting spooked. And I intend to finish reading it while we're here.

She squeezes his hand reassuringly as they pick their way over the rocks to the cove, where a middle-aged man in a black tee shirt sits on a rock, and a young girl, with long curly hair that reaches all the way to the small of her back, plays in the water nearby. Beyond her the shore bends abruptly behind a clump of trees that lean into the water at high tide. There the waters are calmer. As the waves curl up to the shore, they are a transparent blue green. A tawny dog is digging the beach sand as it hunts for crabs, its front legs working a furious fusillade of sand that flies behind it and piles up quickly as though it is building a sand castle. It pauses, contemplates the progress it has made with its ears cocked, barks, and begins digging again. The crab has skittered deeper into the sand.

There are rocks further out in the sea against which the bigger waves break. Beyond that is the open sea. At the point where the cove begins there is almost no sand. It is all rock. The rocks are green with algae and seaweed where mudskippers jump over little pools of clear seawater and twisted roots of trees and fallen branches.

We don't have much time, do we? she asks. He follows her line of sight. She is looking at other people coming towards them from the cove. They are leaving. Less than half an hour, I guess, he says.

They pass four people on their way from the cove. When they reach the cove there is no one else there.

The girl hangs her bag on a tree branch, removes her towel, hangs it on the branch. Where is the camera? he asks. She reaches for her bag, opens it, takes the underwater camera out and gives it to him. Then they wear their snorkelling masks and run into the water hand in hand disengaging to swim out into the sea for about fifty metres. From the surface of the water through their snorkelling masks they can see the sea bed clearly. Two sides of the cove are flanked with rocks on the bottom, and in the centre it is sandy all the way to the beach. Some fish are swimming about. In the rocky bottom they spot a crab. It is scuttling in the sand between two rocks. He pushes his snorkelling mask to his forehead and dives down with the camera and shoots it on video mode. From above the surface, the girl spots a black and yellow tiger fish to her left and signals to her companion who surfaces next to her. She tells him where she saw the fish and he takes a deep breath and dives down again. The tiger fish floats above a rocky crag and seeing the diver approach swivels around and faces him as he points the camera at it in the darkening waters.

He is distracted by the sound of thrashing that comes through the water. The tiger fish turns and is gone. The sounds are louder now, deep sounds of a struggle, amplified by the water. As he looks up he can see the water on the surface, five metres above him, churning and what looks like the loom of a huge crocodile pulling his girlfriend down into the sea. The crocodile has seized her by the shoulders, its entire body twisting this way and that in crazy S shapes. The man quickly rises to the surface where the crocodile has begun to roll in the water with her. He can hear her scream cut through the air like a knife. For a few seconds he is paralysed. The crocodile is huge, more than twice the length of the man and only fifteen metres away. Through the blur of movement, he can see the head of the crocodile and its huge jaws and enormous teeth twisted as if in a vicious grin, and its yellow eyes fixed on him. The man shouts and throws his camera at the crocodile, aiming at the head, hoping to hit its eyes. It misses the head and instead hits the lashing tail of the crocodile. The force flings the camera high into the air. As it falls into the sea the camera spins once and then once more, on video mode; then it splashes into the water and sinks to the bottom, pointing upwards where the crocodile is taking the woman away into the deep, swimming underwater. The man can no longer hear her scream and when he reaches the beach he can no longer see the crocodile. As he runs down the empty beach all the way to the resort to tell them a giant crocodile has taken his girlfriend, the setting sun is staining the sky blood red. At the bottom of the cove the camera continues to film till its battery runs out, the sea pulling it along the bottom as the tide comes in. There is a dog on the beach, barking continuously at the sea.

Nobody believes him. At the hotel, when his companion does not turn up for the night, they think that he has drowned her and call the police. The deputy superintendent of police drives up in his jeep, listens to the story and instructs the man not to leave the island for a few days and takes away his passport saying he will keep it in his custody till the matter is sorted out. The next day they find the towel she had hung on the branch. There is no sign of her bag. Divers look for the camera in the sea bottom around the area where the man indicates the attack took place and boats comb the area for miles. There is no sign of her snorkel either.

On the second day one of the divers sees the strap of the underwater camera snagged on a rock. He finds the camera buried in sand. In the laptop where they download the video they see a crab, a tiger fish, then a whole lot of movement, blurry and out of focus, snatches of sky, intermittent screams, and then underwater shots. They play the video in slow motion and they can see in the corner of some of the frames what appears to be a crocodile's tail, then its front right leg, then a part of a woman's body and once, very briefly, what appears to be the jaws of the crocodile holding the victim. Then there are shots of the sky turning orange, a glimpse of a cloud, the waves of the surface, then the tree line of the cove appears in a corner of the frame, then water, rocks, water. After that all that is seen is the sea turning black.

There has never been a crocodile attack in this area before, at Neil's Cove, in Havelock island. Crocodiles had never been spotted in the area. As the word spreads, they close Beach

Number Seven and intensify patrolling. A couple of policemen walk up and down the length of the beach intermittently to make sure that no one ventures into the sea. A number of times the fishermen and forest department personnel spot a crocodile, fourteen-foot long, swimming close to the cove. On the fourth day at low tide they see the body of a partly eaten woman on the muddy mouth of an estuary around the bend of the Radhanagar beach, and go to retrieve it. As they approach they can hear the high whine of bluebottles taking off and landing on her body lying face down in the mud. They tie a cloth round their faces to block the smell that emanates from the rotting corpse. The right arm is missing. It is bitten clean from the shoulder. When they turn the body over half the girl's face is missing. From the empty sockets maggots wriggle their way out. Most of her hair is missing. The crocodile has eaten a portion of her abdomen and midriff. Her left leg is broken and her nails have turned black.

The forest department issues an order to capture the crocodile. A crocodile catcher from Chennai comes and spends a few days in the area trying to catch the crocodile with nets, gives up and goes away. Some days later they bait the crocodile with the carcass of a stray dog. It takes six men to keep the crocodile down with ropes after it has been shot several times with tranquilizer guns. They wrap its snout firmly with thick yellow ropes. The crocodile is so long that they have to nail two wooden planks together so they can tie the crocodile firmly to it. They tie the legs together and wrap it with gunny sack from the snout to the tail and tie more ropes over the gunny sack running it around the planks. Only its nostrils, which keep opening and closing as it breathes, are exposed. They cover the eyes of the crocodile and board it on a ship to Port Blair to resettle it in the mini zoo on the hilltop over Phoenix Bay overlooking

Sahajeevan Colony. When they measure it is 3.9 metres from the snout to the tail tip. It remains unclear if it is the same crocodile that attacked the woman or another one which has swum from Outram islands eleven nautical miles away, where many crocodiles have been spotted.

On the day the crocodile is caught the man decides to leave Havelock to pick up the threads of his life. That is the day they find the bag the girl had hung on the tree at the cove. A Bengali fisherman out to cast his net from the rocks beyond the cove spies it in a thicket under a badam tree about a kilometre from the beach, off a track winding through the forest. The contents of the bag are strewn around. A long line of red ants swarm on a half-eaten Mars bar. A tube of sun tan lotion lies a couple of metres away from the bag. The toothy end of a green comb sticks out from under a couple of big brown dry mahua leaves. The fisherman picks up the strewn objects and methodically begins to put them into the bag. Everything except the Mars bar. The book she was reading lies under the bag. It is spread open, its spine facing the tree tops. Dew has softened the hardcover. The pages are wet and soiled. The man is illiterate and cannot read the writing on the cover. There is a silhouette of a big fish on the cover, probably a shark, he thinks. As he closes the book and puts it inside the bag a couple of parrots fly away squawking from the badam tree.

Whales in the Rain

That is when Rama Rao Jr spots the whales.

Whale *machchi*, whale *machchi*, he shouts, pointing to the port side. The senior Rama Rao, his brother-in-law, cuts the engines and lets the dinghy drift amidst the waves. The sky is overcast, and darker clouds are gathering. They are coming up from the port bow-side, moving briskly and purposefully in the wind, as though they are warriors headed for battle.

The whales are about five hundred metres from the dinghy. Through the thin drizzle Rama Rao cannot make out the shape of Sir Hugh Rose Island which had been on the stern side. The whales are spouting, the water whooshing up noisily in a gush. Swimming lazily by their side is a pod of dolphins. Their backs glisten as they swim alongside the whales. There are two whales, spouting as they come up to the surface. One of them is big, the other smaller, probably a mother whale and its offspring. They cannot make out what kind of whales these are.

It's my lucky day! Bruno Beauregard shouts. I never thought we would spot whales in this part of the world!

Bruno wants to get them on film.

They wash up sometimes. A baby whale washed up on Ross Island some years ago, the skeleton is in the Marine Museum near my house, says Commander Baath.

But these are live ones, Bruno points out, as he readies his mask, snorkel, fins, his diving tank, and his camera.

Go towards the whales, he instructs, they are harmless. Try to get us as close as possible. I want to take some pictures.

There isn't much light, even though it is only two fifteen in the afternoon. The drone of the dinghy's engines becomes louder as Rama Rao steers towards the whales and the dolphins. When the dinghy approaches the whales and the dolphins, they dive into the sea. The tail fin of the bigger whale rises up in the air when it dives and it looks huge, sea water pouring off it. It dives with a splash they can hear over the waves and the rain. Bruno doesn't know what to do now. Rama Rao stops the engines and everyone looks around for signs of the whales. The waves have become bigger now, their crests specked with white foam and the dinghy is moving around quite a bit now because of the size of the waves. The dolphins surface first, a little to the port side, and then the whales and they begin to spout again.

Go towards them, Bruno Beauregard urges Rama Rao. This time let's circle them from a distance.

The engines start again and Rama Rao steers towards the whales once more. The dinghy begins to circle the whales from a distance of about a hundred metres.

Bruno begins to take pictures. He looks through the viewfinder, clicks a few pictures and shouts, Cut in a little nearer.

As the dinghy comes nearer the whales dive in again. This time they appear much farther away after what seems to be a long time. Bruno asks Rama Rao to steer for them again but when there is still some distance the whales go under once again. When they surface they appear along the side of the starboard and swim away.

Follow them, Bruno says. Rama Rao looks at Commander Baath for instructions. Baath shrugs and says, Do as he says. *Peecha karo*.

Without a word Rama Rao starts one engine and steers behind the whales. They are not going in any particular direction. They go toward one direction and then change their course. For half an hour Rama Rao follows them. The whales then slow down a little and Bruno tells his companion, Camille, Put on your gear, let's swim towards them.

Camille Pascal takes off the blue flower print dress she wears over her bikini and puts on her snorkel, her fins and follows Bruno into the cold sea in the rain. When Bruno and Camille swim the troughs they are not visible. They bob into view with the crests. It is now raining heavier. Baath looks up at the sky, shielding his eyes with his palm to ward off the rain and looks around. Off in the distance the clouds are rumbling and soon there is lightning. Drops of water fall off his beard, wet with rain.

Baath is impatient after a while. Start the engines, let's go fetch them, he tells Rama Rao Sr, who starts one engine, pulling the cord. The engine hesitates then sputters to life, and grey black smoke curls up from the exhaust. As they approach Bruno and Camille, Baath shouts out to them. Rama Rao cuts the engines and the two start swimming towards the dinghy.

Forget it, Baath shouts, leaning over the side of the dinghy as Bruno and Camille push up their masks. It is not going to work. We are not going to be able to get near them. They are very shy and the sound of the engines is disturbing them and now it's too dark. We have to head back to Port Blair. I don't like the way the weather is turning. We better leave right away.

The dinghy is bobbing up and down in the water. The ladder

on the side, clamped to the railing of the boat, rises and falls with the waves, its lowest rung, the fifth, touches the water now and then. Bruno and Camille look at each other, say something in French and clamber aboard grasping the ladder. As they come up Rama Rao Jr helps them up, first Camille, then Bruno. Camille, tall and willowy, removes her snorkelling mask, gives her head a shake and smoothes back her blond hair which comes to the nape. Then she removes her fins, and diving tanks. Bruno grunts at his companion, pushes his snorkelling mask out of his head and runs his palm over his head which looks clean shaven except for a fringe of close cropped hair in the back of his head that looks like an atoll.

The current's too strong, says Camille, reaching for the towel which is already wet. She moves to her seat in front of the dinghy, a plank that runs on one side, under the canvas awning. There she towels herself and Bruno picks his way to the plank placed opposite.

There is no sign of the whales now. Visibility has dropped some more. Even though it is only about three in the afternoon it looks as though it is past sunset.

Rama Rao, Baath shouts. Start both the engines. Head straight for Port Blair.

Baath depends on Rama Rao a lot. He has been sailing for most of his adult life in these waters. He doesn't need to give Rama Rao directions to Port Blair, which is twenty nautical miles west of Sir Hugh Rose.

Fine sir, says Rama Rao and takes a course. He looks around to get his bearings. He cannot spot any island. He steers the boat so that it is going against the current, against the sea. *Kuch maloom nahin chal raha hai*, he tells Himanshu who is sitting next to him. Himanshu says nothing.

There is lightning everywhere now. Rain comes down heavily in sheets. There is no sign of Sir Hugh Rose Island. It has disappeared as if it was never there. The dinghy has followed the whales round and round and now there is no telling how to get a bearing due west. Baath knows that it doesn't really matter if Rama Rao heads north of Port Blair. Whatever you do don't go south of Port Blair, he tells Rama Rao.

Fine, says Rama Rao Sr, steering the prow of the dinghy against the current.

The rumble of thunder is now constant. Baath has never seen lightning so close. Big bolts of lightning strike all around the dinghy. Baath can see Bruno and Camille hug each other. Bruno is saying something into her ears. She looks scared. Baath is no stranger to thunder, but now in the middle of the sea with both the engines running he is afraid that a bolt of lightning might strike the dinghy. It gets worse and a bolt plunges into the black sea right behind the boat. The thunder that follows is so loud that Camille covers her ears and begins to cry. Her face is white in the lightning. It is raining so heavily now that visibility is down to two metres. From where he is sitting with Himanshu Mallick, Rama Rao Sr can barely see Baath.

The wind carries Camille's sobbing to where the others are sitting. All of them can hear it clearly now. Bruno wraps a wet towel round her and tries to console her. Everyone is wet in the rain and the waves are now gushing into the boat. Normally, in an hour about six or seven litres of water collect in the dinghy because of the small holes in the wood, made by insects. Now the waves that crash on the boat bring buckets full of water inside. Rama Rao Jr begins to bail out the water with a plastic jerry can that has been cut to work like a bailer. Through the howling wind and the din of the rain and the lightning and thunder,

Baath can hear Camille's sobs. She sounds like a little girl. Her shoulders are heaving intermittently. Bruno looks around and wonders if the boat is going in the right direction. Half an hour passes and he becomes restless.

Baath senses his restlessness. He tells Bruno not to worry. Rama Rao is here and he is taking us in the correct direction. He knows. He has been a fisherman all his life. He knows these waters.

The sea is against the boat. The sea was against the boat when Rama Rao took direction for Port Blair. Once a seaman takes direction he knows how to stick to it. Sometimes when a storm brews up, the sea gets confused and rough. The wind comes from one side and the waves from the other. The swells come from both the sides. Baath knows that once a course is taken over a distance of twenty miles maybe Rama Rao will go out one or two miles here or there.

Bruno looks worried. He reaches for the regulator of his diving tank. Bruno has been using his own regulator he had brought from Mauritius, with Baath's diving tanks and equipment. His regulator has a magnetic compass in it. Normally a regulator apart from the breathing piece, shows the air pressure in the tank and the depth as well. Bruno's regulator has a pressure gauge, a depth gauge as well as a magnetic compass. He studies the compass for a while.

Then he looks at Baath and says, I think Rama Rao is going in the wrong direction. According to my compass we need to be going that way, he says pointing at the opposite direction.

Baath responds politely, Look here Bruno, I really trust Rama Rao. There is no reason for me to not trust him. He will take us in the correct direction. You don't worry.

But no, Bruno responds. You really have to look at my

compass. He comes over to where Baath is sitting and shows him the compass.

Baath looks at it. Very nice, he says. But we don't know this compass at all. How old is this compass? How regularly have you been using it? When did you last calibrate it to check its correctness? After all, Baath thinks, this is a magnetic compass, which is near a metal tank, and all this may cause some deviation.

Bruno looks exasperated. He gets up, goes to Camille Pascal. Baath can hear him talking in French with her. Both of them keep looking at the compass and gesticulating, as if they are talking to the compass and the compass is talking back to them. A little later Bruno comes back to Baath and says, You know, my girlfriend is very worried. She is hoping that you are not taking us in the wrong direction.

Why would I want to do that? I also want to get home, you know? I have my wife and kids to think about. The others here also have their families.

No, no, no, I know. But she is very worried.

So, what do you want me to do?

I think we should go as per my compass.

Do you know how to read your compass?

Yes of course! It is my compass! isn't it?

Damn good! If you are very worried and your girlfriend is very worried that we may be taking you in the wrong direction, why don't you go sit down with Rama Rao there and tell him where to steer? If you don't trust me or him, you take charge.

Bruno looks at Camille Pascal who doesn't say anything. He goes to where Rama Rao Sr is and shows him the compass.

Rama Rao doesn't look at the compass. He does not understand compasses. He is a fisherman who goes by island features, currents and the stars at night. He looks at Commander Baath. When Bruno asks him to change course, Rama Rao hands over the tiller to Rama Rao Jr and comes up to Baath.

Sir, he is telling me to go in a different direction, what should I do?

Rama Rao, our guest thinks you are going in the wrong direction. I have told him I trust you but he says that his compass is right and you are going in the wrong direction.

Main kya karoon? What should I do?

Tum batao tumko kya karna hai. If you are hundred per cent sure you are going in the right direction, you tell him not to worry. But if you have the smallest doubt in your mind about your direction then you listen to him.

It is not a question of having doubt, sir. When we left Chota Neil this was the best course in my mind and I think we can reach Port Blair if we keep going in this direction. I took a course against the current, keeping Chota Neil behind my back. It is not a question of doubt.

Rama Rao, we went round and round when we saw the whales, didn't we? Certainly anybody can make a mistake. He says his compass is very good. It is genuine. You should go by that compass.

But sir…

Commander Baath is suddenly angry. He shouts, You are the dinghymaster and I am the captain. I am telling you to go and tell him to take over if you have the slightest doubt, the slightest of doubt, do you understand?

Okay sir, I will tell him we'll go wherever he tells me to go.

Rama Rao goes back to the tiller. Baath can see that Rama Rao is angry. He listens to Bruno who is giving him a new course. Bruno's course is with the current. As the dinghy eases into the current, it begins to speed along. Rama Rao is uneasy. He knows that to get to Chota Neil you come straight with the current and when you head back to Port Blair you go against the current. It is a little difficult to negotiate the waves coming at you. Now he has no difficulty negotiating. The dinghy is going along fast, riding the waves.

Baath pulls his cap over his face and leans against the backrest of the plank on the far side of Camille Pascal, stretches out his legs, and closes his eyes. The cap covers the frowns on his forehead. He thinks that they have gone on for about half an hour after the whales. In an hour or an hour and half, they should be able to see signs of Port Blair. Maybe two hours maximum. That is, if they are headed in the right direction. It is already dark and there is every possibility that by the time they got near Port Blair, they would not be able to see the loom of it. There is a light house over there, though, the North Point Light House. It is a powerful light house. On a clear night it could be seen from twenty nautical miles away and a visual fix could be obtained. In the rain they would probably see it ten miles off. If not ten miles they would see it five miles off. Or even three miles at the very least. In that distance they should get some hint of land.

Bruno and Camille Pascal sit close to each other for the next half hour. They talk to each other now and then. Baath doesn't know French but he can make out the worry in their voices. Himanshu moves next to Rama Rao Sr and sits by his side, by the tiller. Both of them are talking in Bengali.

We are going in the wrong direction, Rama Rao Sr tells Himanshu.

Did you tell Commander Baath?

He asked me if I was captain or was he the captain. He was angry.

Himanshu says nothing. A little towards the bow, on the plank that runs athwart the dinghy, Rama Rao Jr is taking a break from bailing. He is chewing on his *sukka*. He keeps spitting some of it out from time to time, leaning over the dinghy, into the sea. He doesn't look bothered if they are going in the right direction or not. He chews his *sukka* silently.

They keep going on this course for almost two hours. Baath adjusts his cap, looks around and cannot see any light anywhere. There is no sign of the lighthouse. There is no sign of any landfall either. Just the rain and the sound of the engines. He shouts: *Arre* Rama Rao *abhi tak kuch dikhayi nahin de raha hai kya*? Where are we now?

Rama Rao Sr glares at Baath and shouts back: You can forget Port Blair, you can forget Andamans also. We do not know where we are. If you had not shown us the wrong way, we would have reached home by now. I would have been sleeping in my home by now.

Baath ignores the anger and goes across to Bruno and tells him, We will have to stop now.

Why? What happened? Bruno asks. He looks both vaguely defiant and worried. Rain water keeps running down his clean shaven head.

We have run for two hours, Baath responds. There should have been some sign somewhere of the lights, the glow, the loom of Port Blair. There has been no sign at all of anything. If we are going in the wrong direction then after some time we will be even farther in the wrong direction than we are now. That is why we have to stop now and wait.

No. No we can't stop. We have to keep going. My compass

is right. We are not making much headway because of the weather.

Rama Rao can hear them arguing but since they are talking in English he cannot make out exactly what they are arguing about. Himanshu understands enough English to make out that there is a serious disagreement brewing. Bruno goes across to Camille and speaks to her in French. Camille who has been silent for a while now says something and begins to cry. Bruno comes back to Baath and says, We have to continue.

We should drop anchor and wait for the skies to clear up. Then we can get some bearing and proceed. Baath is standing his ground now.

Bruno keeps going back to Camille and keeps returning to Baath to urge him to stay the course. Baath finally gets fed up and shouts to Rama Rao to throw the anchor down.

Which one should I throw, Rama Rao asks.

The heavier one, Baath shouts. But throw it after adding all the line you have.

There are two anchors in the dinghy. One is a very small anchor with three hooks, which was used if there was no float to tie the dinghy to. The smaller anchor does not grip rocks at the bottom in a manner that can cause damage. It is easier to prise it from the rocks below. The heavier anchor is for emergencies. It has more than hundred metres of line on it.

Rama Rao stops the engines, and the boat begins to drift in the swift current. He adds the extra line to the heavy anchor, secures one end to the dinghy, and heaves it overboard. The anchor goes down with a splash and all the line, more than a hundred and fifty metres of it, gets played out quickly. The anchor doesn't touch the bottom. The dinghy keeps drifting.

Baath now knows there is something amiss. The anchor

hadn't reached the bottom. If they were going back from Chota Neil to Port Blair and if they had already covered half the distance, the depth should not have been more than fifty or sixty metres. He did this route almost daily on the bigger passenger liner that he captained between Havelock Island and Port Blair, the *Bambooka*. The waters south of Neil were far deeper. Baath knows that the waters to the North of Neil were not so deep, and the anchor would have touched bottom there too. So they had not travelled north either.

Let the anchor be in the water, Baath tells Rama Rao. With the heavier anchor dragging in the water, the rate of the drift would slow down.

Till we are sure of what direction we are moving toward, I am not going to pull up the anchor. I am not going to start the engines till we are sure of the direction, Baath tells Bruno, who puts his arms around Camille. She is crying again.

Baath then comes up to Himanshu and smiles at him.

Happy birthday Himanshu. Baath is smiling. You are not going to forget this birthday for a long time to come, Baath tells Himanshu.

Himanshu is not smiling. He is thinking of his parents. He hasn't told them he was going with Baath. He thinks of the *kwasha* chicken his mother promised to make him for his birthday. He is suddenly hungry. He begins to think he picked the wrong day for a joyride.

The dinghy drifts amidst the big waves into the mighty black night, the rain tumbling incessantly from the sky.

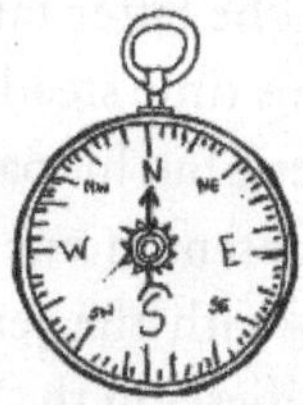

Islands in a Stream

Camille is sleeping on the plank that runs along the port side of the dinghy. A wet Bay Island Hotel towel covers her torso upto her neck. It is spread lengthwise over her. Her legs below the calves lie exposed. Bruno is lying on the plank opposite. Himanshu is on the floor between the two. Baath is sitting on the plank, unable to sleep. He looks up at the dark sky. It shows no sign of clearing. The thick clouds hang low. Rama Rao Sr is at the tiller. Rama Rao Jr sleeps with the tarpaulin pulled over him. It is raining intermittently.

Baath lies down on the plank facing the sky . He is looking for breaks in the clouds to see if he can spot the moon. Once, between the patches of clouds, he briefly spies the moon. It is a half moon which slowly moves behind a cloud. It is directly above the dinghy now. He cannot make out if it is rising or setting.

Baath is uncomfortably wet. The wind blows cold over him. He sits up and reaches below the plank, takes out a spare t shirt he has brought along and wears it on top of the one he is already wearing, careful not to disturb Himanshu who is now curled up against the plank.

It is two thirty now and Rama Rao hands over the tiller to Rama Rao Jr and wakes Himanshu up and goes to sleep where

Himanshu was sleeping. The latter takes a bailer and begins to bail. It is raining again, this time steadily.

Baath longs for a cigarette but his packet is drenched. Around five the sky begins to brighten on one side. Baath wakes Rama Rao Sr. Fill the tank up with the jerrycan fuel, he instructs. Rama Rao Jr empties the diesel in the jerrycan into the tank.

Anchor *uthalo*, Baath instructs further. Raise the anchor. Start both the engines. Keep going west and keep the sun behind you.

Baath thinks that even if they have drifted south due west they would still reach some island or the other. If they were already south of Port Blair, there was Rutland further south, then Cinq Island, then North Brother, South Brother, and Little Andaman. There was a string of land out there. It stretched seventy miles from Port Blair all the way to Little Andaman.

There is no sign of the sun yet, and through the clouds a weak, grey light suffuses the air. All around the sea looks like molten lead. Rama Rao Sr pulls in the anchor as Himanshu coils the anchor line. The thud of the anchor on the dinghy floor wakes Bruno. He gets up and looks around. He watches Rama Rao Sr start the engines and then he looks at the direction where the sun is rising behind the clouds.

Just check if the sun is rising in the correct direction, Baath tells Bruno. Bruno reaches for the regulator to check his compass. Camille has woken up too. She watches Bruno as he looks silently at the compass and shakes it and looks at it then shakes it again. He keeps quiet.

Should I ask Rama Rao to go by your compass again or should he go by the sun? Baath asks. Bruno ignores the taunt. Finally he says, My compass is wrong.

What? How can it be? This is the compass that you trusted? This is the compass that you swore was genuine.

Camille sits up and starts shouting at Bruno in French. He tries to placate her, reaching out to her. She slaps his hand away and turns the other way. Baath can see that she is furious.

Okay, let's forget it, Baath says. We now know where the sun is. Let us go back home.

The dinghy ploughs its way through the waves. The sea is picking up. The waves are now two metres high and rising. The dinghy is pitching and rolling. The waves are coming in from the southwest and west. Even with both engines running the dinghy is hardly moving forward. It is as if it is suspended between the waves that lift it up and then set it down. The dinghy is going up, climbing the wave and then dipping down. It is making more headway sideways. Baath is worried about the fuel position. He has modified the tank to hold forty litres of diesel. In addition, the dinghy carried a jerry can of thirty litres. Each engine consumed three litres of fuel an hour. On a calm sea the dinghy could do about twelve knots with both engines running. It has run three hours to Neil, then another four hours after that.

How much diesel do we have left, Rama Rao? asks Baath.

Only ten litres left sir, replies Rama Rao Sr checking the fuel position.

Shut down one engine then, orders Baath.

Rama Rao shuts down one engine. With only one engine running the dinghy is practically at standstill. After a while Baath asks Rama Rao to start the other engine as well. The progress is agonizingly slow. Around eight twenty Himanshu who is sitting on the prow spots two bits of land in the far distance. Baath peers into the distance and says, The bigger one could be Rutland. It has the third highest peak in the Andamans. The other one is probably South Cinq.

Everybody is excited. Camille hugs Bruno. Himanshu shouts in joy.

Baath is happy. He reaches for his cigarettes. They are shapeless and wet so he throws them away. He asks Camille if she has a cigarette. She fishes her packet out but that is wet too. Baath's lighter has stopped working. So has Camille's. Rama Rao is the only other smoker on board. He smokes beedis. He fishes out a packet of beedis. There are only two left. Somehow he has managed to keep them dry.

If you don't mind, Rama Rao says, we can share a beedi each.

Damn good! says Baath.

Rama Rao Sr takes a matchbox which is dry too and lights his beedi after a few attempts. He then cups the flame and tries to light Baath's. The flame dies out. He strikes another match. This time the beedi lights up. Baath draws deeply on the beedi and lets the smoke out very slowly. They are all looking at the islands that draw nearer and nearer almost imperceptibly. Baath thinks they must be seven or eight miles away at the most. At the rate they were progressing, about a little more than an hour and a quarter away. Gradually they can see it more clearly. It is Rutland Island in the distance.

Suddenly one diesel engine begins to choke and sputter. It finally stops. The other engine still has some diesel left. Baath wonders how much longer the diesel will last. Shortly after nine in the morning, the second engine also begins to sputter and dies. They have run out of diesel. All the dinghy has left is a ten litre jerrycan of engine oil, kept in case the oil leaked out for some reason.

Drop the anchor, shouts Baath. Drop it now. Play out all

the line. Baath knows the gradients from those islands are very steep.

Rama Rao throws the anchor overboard. Rapidly the line follows till it is all played out. Baath assumes the depth here must be more than 300 metres. There is no more rope in the dinghy to reach that kind of depth.

The sea is becoming rough. The waves are rising now. With the engine shut, the boat is turning on its own, parallel to the giant waves. As the bigger waves rush in water starts crashing into the dinghy from the side. There is a chance that the dinghy might capsize. There are two long oars in the dinghy. Baath asks Rama Rao Sr to pull them out and they begin rowing. The boat remains parallel to the waves. There is no difference at all. The waves and the wind keep pushing the boat back, away from the island. They are drifting at the rate of half a knot. They can see the islands recede in the distance. By afternoon they can no longer see the islands.

Baath feels hungry but there is no food left. All the food that was left has gone soggy in the rain and the waves crashing into the dinghy. They have some fishing lines and a lure but fish don't bite when the sea is rough. The dinghy needed to move much faster to lure the fish. At half a knot the fish wouldn't bite even if the sea were calm. The dinghy is being tossed by the waves, away into the open sea. Water is continuously rushing into the boat. Himanshu, Baath, and both the Rama Raos are all taking turns emptying the water out with the three bailers in the dinghy. They can't even correct the direction of the boat with the oars because the winds are too strong. There is nothing they can do. If they let the boat carry on like this it is sure to capsize. Bruno and Camille are watching helplessly, despair written on their faces.

We have no choice but to rig up a sail, Baath tells Bruno. If we go with the wind there's a much better chance of the boat not capsizing, Baath shouts over the howling wind.

But if we go with the wind we are going to be heading even farther away from land, Bruno protests.

If the boat capsizes we will be in the water, Baath shouts. We can hang on longer if we are in the dinghy than if we are in the water. The only way we can stay in the boat is if we go with the wind. Bruno keeps quiet.

Take down the canvas from the front of the boat, Baath shouts to Himanshu and Rama Rao Sr. Quickly. We have no time to lose.

Himanshu, Rama Rao and Baath begin to dismantle the tarpaulin top that covers the front portion of the dinghy under which Camille and Bruno shelter. It is tough work. The dinghy is rocking from side to side against the big waves. It is moving so much that it is difficult to stand and work.

Baath instructs Rama Rao to remove two of the wooden poles that support the tarpaulin lengthwise. These are long poles and Baath thinks they can form the side-supports for the makeshift sail.

Now tie the poles to the two sides of the canopy, instructs Baath. Tie it to the sides that have the holes in them. The canopy has a line of evenly placed metal-ringed holes running on two sides. Using the rope in the dinghy they tie the canopy to the poles. They try putting the poles through the interstices of the wooden beams that support the hull like a skeleton on the inside of the dinghy but it doesn't hold. They try supporting it with another stick in the narrower end. Even that doesn't hold. Finally Baath instructs that the other end of the canopy be tied down to a gap in the beams in the aft section of the dinghy.

This works. It is tough work tying it because the improvised sail immediately fills with wind. Rama Rao runs to the tiller to steer with the wind. The dinghy begins to go with the sea. It is moving faster now, the sail filled with wind.

Soon huge waves start rushing in from the back of the dinghy. The dinghy plows into the trough and the stern sticks out in the front. The waves are so big that Himanshu feels the boat will be submerged. But the dinghy rides the waves.

It is almost evening now and it is still raining. They drink small quantities of water. They are not thirsty. They are hungry. Bruno has two bananas left in his carry bag. He takes one and shares it with Camille. The other banana remains in the bag. They don't offer it to anyone. Bruno offers the first bite to Camille and eats what is left of it. After eating, he puts the banana peel back into the bag. Camille can feel the rest of them staring. She opens her bag and takes out three chewing gums. She offers one to Baath who takes it silently, puts it in his mouth and begins chewing on it. Thank you, he says after a while. You know I've never eaten chewing gum for lunch. I must say it is much better than I thought it would be. Camille smiles weakly at Baath.

Rama Rao Sr takes out the vadas that have become soggy in the rain and is about to eat them. Baath makes him throw them away. He doesn't want anybody getting sick in the dinghy.

Baath instructs Rama Rao Sr to pull the ladder hooked to the side of the dinghy inside. Rama Rao leans it on the plank.

The dinghy is surging east in the wind. Baath thinks that if they continue in this direction they will wash up in the southern coast of Burma or the northern coast of Thailand. But that was still about 200 or 220 nautical miles away.

It is as if Bruno has read Baath's thoughts.

Land is very far away this way, Bruno tells Baath.

At least we are not going towards India, Baath responds. That coastline is 700 miles away.

The Open Sea

Baath hopes to ride out the storm and go with the wind. At the speed of a little over half a knot, if the wind kept up in the same direction it would take a little over twenty days for the dinghy to reach Thailand or Burma. Baath knows that it is not such a simple proposition. From whatever he has heard of Burma, Baath figures that they are safer out in the sea. It might well be that they could get thrown into a lockup and forgotten and nobody would ever come to know. Or worse still they may fall into the hands of the Burmese poachers, like the ones from whom the dinghy had been captured. Their fate would be worse than death. Baath tells himself that there are many ships that sail between Port Blair and Little Andaman, between Port Blair and Nicobar, both ways. Maybe one would cross them and they would get picked up. But the bigger worry was: Would they make it alive?

Baath hears Camille sobbing again and looks at her. Bruno is murmuring something soothing into her ears. A flash of lightning lights up the sea. Baath can see Himanshu is disturbed. There is another flash and then another. Thunder follows. Baath goes over to Himanshu and asks him what he's thinking of.

I am worried about my mother.

Are you worried about your mother or are you missing her cooking here?

That too, Himanshu replies, trying to ignore the hunger. Don't worry, by the time you get back home your mother would have learnt a couple of new dishes. Everything will be fine. Why don't you go and help Rama Rao Jr bail the water? *Arre Rama Rao woh line lagao machchi pakadne ke liye.* Get the line ready to catch fish, Rama Rao.

Saab raat ho raha hai. We are going very slowly. Fish won't bite in the night.

Kya pata? Line lagao to sahi. Kya jaata lagane mein? Throw out the fishing line. You never know what will bite.

Baath asks for some water. Rama Rao Sr passes him the bottle. There is hardly more than a mouthful left in the second two litre bottle of mineral water. They are now without food and almost without water.

It is raining heavily now. The squalls keep coming. But there are no containers on board to store water. Baath realizes that it is going to take some days for them to reach land. To remain alive they have to collect water to drink.

What should we do now? Baath shouts above the gusting wind to Bruno. We can't store water in the jerry can because there is fuel in it. We can't store it in the bailers because we need them to bail the water out.

Well, we can start by filling the mineral water bottles, can't we?

That's only four litres. How far can that take us?

What do you propose then?

Baath looks at the diving tanks near Rama Rao Sr. There are six on board. Each has a capacity of carrying twelve litres.

What if we open up the diving tanks and fill them with water as well? Baath asks.

Bruno is thoughtful for a while. We should fill only three tanks, he says.

Why do you say that? If we are able to open the necks of all six we should fill water in all of them, don't you think? That way we will have more water. It will last us longer.

I don't agree. Where we are headed there are a lot of pirates. We have diving equipment on board. We have a woman on board. If we should encounter them then the three of us can go underwater – you, me and Camille. We can escape by going underwater only if we open three tanks. Not all of them.

Baath is flabbergasted.

What is going to happen to the other three in that case?

Bruno shrugs his shoulders.

That is not fair. They are my boys. How can we leave them to the mercy of pirates? This doesn't make any sense to me at all. How long will you stay underwater with these tanks? One hour? What happens after that?

Himanshu and Rama Rao start opening up all the diving tanks. We are going to fill them all with water, Baath orders. Rama Rao Sr hands over the tiller to Baath and opens the tool box that is kept by the engine. It has spanners and other tools to maintain the engine. Some of the diving tanks hadn't been opened for a while and the necks have jammed. The spanner keeps slipping off the necks, which have got rounded. One by one they open the necks of the tanks. They open it little by little so the air inside escapes at a slow rate. If they release the air quickly then moisture would form inside the tank and it would begin to rust. The air escapes with a hiss. In the end they are able to open only three of the tanks. Bruno looks relieved. Camille has stopped talking altogether. She does not talk to Bruno, nor does she talk to Baath. She looks morose.

Baath asks for the smaller mineral water bottle that Bay Island hotel has given Bruno. It is a one-litre bottle. Baath tells Rama Rao Sr to cut the bottle in half. Now there are two halves, a container and a funnel. They use the smaller tarpaulin that covers the stern of the dinghy to catch rain water. Himanshu, Baath, Rama Rao Sr and Bruno hold the tarpaulin at each of the ends. They don't stretch it but allow it to slack at the centre so water can collect. Then using the funnel end of the bottle they channel the water into the three tanks one after the other and the two two-litre mineral water bottles.

It is late in the night by the time the last bottle is filled. Camille has been keeping quiet. She tells Bruno something in French. Looking worried Bruno comes up to Baath and says, There is a crisis.

What kind of a crisis, asks Baath. Behind Bruno, Baath can see Camille looking at him. She looks uncomfortable.

Camille has got her period. She was not supposed to get it till next week. They were not due. Maybe it's the weather. Maybe it's the stress. What do we do?

It is a crisis, says Baath, looking around the dinghy. There is no privacy in the dinghy. Camille was wearing a bikini and a short dress over it and a tee shirt as well. But that tee shirt became too wet to wear and she has put it away.

Give me one of the towels, Baath asks Bruno. Bruno gives the one he has been using to cover himself. Baath asks Rama Rao for a knife and cuts the towel into thin strips so they can be used as sanitary napkins. It has to last Camille at least seven days, if worst came to worst.

Give these to Camille to use, he tells Bruno. Then he instructs Bruno to use the other towel as a screen so Camille can have a little privacy and clean up as well.

Give her one of the mineral water bottles, says Baath. At least it's still raining. We will be able to fill it again later.

While Bruno stands holding the towel like a screen, Baath assigns duties for the rest of them. One person at the tiller, one person bailing, and one person catching up on sleep. Because it is still raining he encourages them to drink water. But nobody is thirsty.

Baath is sitting at the tiller chewing the gum Camille has given him. He has chewed all day on it and his jaws are hurting. He removes the gum from his mouth and sticks it under the plank on which Rama Rao sits to steer the dinghy. Lightning strikes some way off. Baath sees the waves rise behind him like small hills, the crests foaming white in the heaving, black open sea. Himanshu is bailing water. He keeps a lookout for ships that pass in the night.

No ships cross the dinghy that night.

Missing

When Mona Baath woke up on the morning of March 11, a little after seven thirty, Baath had already left for the dive. She remembered him telling her the previous night that he was going to dive off Hugh Rose with Bruno Beauregard and his girlfriend. They didn't normally go to Sir Hugh Rose Island to dive. But Bruno had said he didn't want to dive in the usual spots. Sir Hugh Rose was less frequented by divers. Mona woke Karan and Aman and went about her chores. Both her elder sons were in the midst of examinations. Karan was nine, Amman six, and Nishant the youngest, still sleeping, was one. Normally Baath would go to Wandoor to pick up water, fruits, soft drink and some food along the way. This time he was supposed to have set off from Bay Island hotel in Port Blair. The days he went off to dive Baath usually returned at six thirty or seven in the evening. He would go to his office in Aberdeen Bazaar before he came home. He maintained a room there where he kept all the records of the bookings for the boats he ran to Ross Island and Jolly Buoy. There was an accountant and a couple of helpers. Himanshu worked there as well. If Baath didn't go diving he would walk for an hour in the evening along the promenade near Aberdeen Jetty. He would walk briskly all the way past the Government College grounds, the South Point

Circuit house, along the rocky beach, and follow the curve of the road which sloped up the hill near the small south Indian style temple and then walk all the way back.

It was sometime after five that evening that the storm started brewing. Mona was in the hammock set up in the verandah, listening to old Hindi songs and singing along softly when leaves from the tall tree by the side of the building next to her began to rustle and fly off in the wind, rolling across the verandah and whirling over the vehicles parked outside. She looked up and saw the sky turn dark grey. Without warning the first big drops of rain began to fall. Mona knew it would soon turn into a downpour. She switched off the walkman and pulled herself carefully out of the low yellow hammock, one end of which was tied to the railing of the stairs which led downstairs to the road and the other end to the railing of the verandah. It was so low that when Mona lay in the hammock, it swung gently barely four inches off the ground. Nishant was crawling along the verandah. Mona knew he would go to the plywood partition door, that blocked his passage to the stairs, stand up, and try to open it to go down to the road outside where his brothers played. Baath had got a carpenter to make this swinging plywood partition to prevent stray dogs from sleeping in the verandah whenever it rained. Mona could hear her children's shouts as she leaned over the railing. Karan and Aman were cycling furiously on the road below. They were oblivious to the storm. As she called out to them, the rain was already curving into the verandah and her face and hands were now getting wet. Over the heavy patter of rain she shouted at them to come home immediately. Nishant was now shaking the plywood partition saying, *Baba baba*. As she picked Nishant up from the floor and carried him to the drawing room to switch on the television for him to watch, the wind began rattling the windows and the pages of the magazine she had left on the table in the drawing room began to rustle and flutter. Mona rushed inside to get a towel for Karan and Aman. Then she began to close the windows in the drawing room. She could hear the boys racing up the stairs. Karan, please leave your shoes outside, Mona shouted, even as the boys trooped into the room. Mona sighed as she saw the floor smudged full of wet, muddy footprints. Lightning streaked across the sky intermittently and through the window they looked like electric centipedes crawling past the glass panes into the darkening night. The wind was so strong that it felt as if it was going to rip the windows off their hinges. The distant rumble of thunder drew nearer. The front door slammed shut and opened, swinging wildly. Mona rushed to close the door.

She knew that Baath would have a tough time coming in with the storm. She wondered if Bruno had got his photographs. He had wanted to photograph giant manta rays and dugongs. Mona had never seen a dugong although Baath had seen them on a couple of occasions, though not off Sir Hugh Rose, gently grazing on the sea grass off Rutland Island. Baath didn't return in the evening. Nor did he return later in the night. Mona figured maybe Baath saw the storm roll up and took the dinghy to Havelock or Neil Island to wait out the storm. As she locked up for the night after dinner, Mona expected Baath to be back the next day. At the very least, she thought, he would certainly call.

The next morning Baath hadn't come back home. Neither had he called. Noon came and went and there was still no sign of her husband. By late afternoon Mona began to wonder what had happened to him. She didn't want to share her worries with the children. In the afternoon she called Commander Ashwini

Kumar, the director of shipping services. Mona told him that Baath hadn't come back from his diving trip off Sir Hugh Rose Island. He hadn't called either. Ashwini Kumar knew about the trip. Baath had sounded out both him and Mona for the trip at the Naval Officer's Club the night before the dive. Ashwini had asked him when he was going for the dive with his guests. Baath had said seven in the morning. Ashwini had told him seven was too early for him on a Sunday. He asked Baath if he could start off at nine or nine thirty. If that were possible he would also come along for the trip and he would love to swim off Sir Hugh Rose and dive a bit. But Baath had said it had all been fixed. The timing couldn't be changed. It would throw everything out of schedule. Ashwini had then told him that he would come along the next time. He had forgotten about the dive afterwards.

Now Mona was telling him that Baath hadn't returned. He told her to calm down and that he would take care of it. He first called his office and put out a message to all the police stations to report if they hear a dinghy has landed anywhere in their jurisdiction. The message went out to Neil, Havelock, Baratang, Diglipur. Then he called up the coast guard DIG S.K. Dey, the regional commander of Coast Guard to alert him. The next day the police stations reported that no dinghy fitting the description had been washed ashore. Neither had they got any reports of his whereabouts. Ashwini called Mona to tell her that it appeared Baath could still be at sea. The Coast Guard, the Navy as well as the directors of the shipping services that were plying in the area now knew about the missing dinghy. They were all instructed to look out for it.

DIG S.K. Dey called Mona and she went over with Dey the same information she had given Ashwini. Dey asked if there was a possibility that Baath could have changed the plans. Mona replied that normally didn't happen. If Baath had a plan, he went according to it. As far as Mona knew there was no deviation from the plan. Baath must have headed for Sir Hugh Rose.

Dey thanked her and hung up. He then alerted various agencies, including the air force, on the missing dinghy and advised them of the next steps. A combined search was launched deploying four ships, helicopters and aircraft to look for the missing dinghy. The 745 Squadron of the Coast Guard counted among its assets one Dornier and one Chetak helicopter. CG 766 the Dornier had in the previous three months helped apprehend 26 boats and trawlers. In all, over 170 poachers had been in these boats in the exclusive economic zone illegally.

Squadron Commander V.K. Awasthy was at home when he got a call from the Duty Staff Officer at the Coast Guard Regional Headquarters who told him that a dinghy with Commander Baath had been missing since the previous evening. Their last presumed position was 20 nautical miles east of Port Blair. Awasthi called H.S. Walia and S. Chopra, his Deputy Commandants and made plans to begin the search. The three of them met in the Operations Room.

The searches went on right to the edge of the economic zone, which was 220 nautical miles. They didn't go very much beyond that because there was no knowing how the neighbouring countries would react. Dey got his team to pore over the meteorological information they had, factored in the prevailing winds, currents and tides. They determined that since Baath and his guests had gone diving near Havelock, and if for some reason the engines of the dinghy was not working, given that monsoon was in full play both the wind and the tide may have taken the dinghy in a south westerly direction.

Accordingly the aircraft began searching the eastern side and the south eastern side and went all the way to the south western fringes. The ships were deployed in the area too. By the time the searches began the weather had turned worse. In the operation room all they got were weather updates. It was raining heavily.

On the third day after Baath went missing the Dornier found a small window of opportunity to take off amidst the heavy rain, searching along a southwest direction towards Brother and Sister Islands. By the time they reached the spot the weather turned so bad and the visibility became so poor with the thick mass of clouds and the blinding rain that the aircraft turned back to Port Blair.

In the Water

The rain has let up a bit. The sky brightens across the bow of the dinghy. It is a dull steel grey. Baath scans the skies for signs of change in the weather. The clouds are still massed thick in every corner of the sky. The sea glistens darkly, the foaming waves rush at the dinghy. The weather has held for a quarter of an hour. When Baath is satisfied that it is not going to rain for a while, he pulls out the charts from his bag that is placed under the plank Camille is sleeping on. He spreads it on the plank and tells Himanshu to hold two of the sides so it doesn't fly off in the wind. The rustle of the charts wakes Bruno and he looks around. He removes his tee shirt and wrings it over the prow. Then he shakes it repeatedly and spreads it on the plank he has been lying on so it can dry. He changes his mind and hangs it on the frame of the tarpaulin. It begins to flutter in the stiff winds. The waves smash against the dinghy throwing spray high into the air which keeps falling on them. He studies the chart for a while then rolls it up and puts it away. Himanshu looks for a clue as to what Baath is thinking. But behind his beard, Baath's face remains inscrutable. Then Bruno begins to shout, My tee shirt! My tee shirt, Merde! Baath turns around and looks. Bruno's tee shirt is no longer where he spread it out to dry; the wind has snatched it off the tarpaulin frame and is carrying it away. The tee shirt twists about in the wind and plummets into the sea. There it floats absurdly. As the dinghy rises in the waves they can see the tee shirt briefly as it draws away. Bruno looks upset. Thinking that Bruno might jump into the sea to retrieve it, Baath gives Bruno his own second tee shirt which he has been wearing to ward off the cold. Bruno takes it and puts it on immediately.

The wind blows much stronger now and the sail is making a fluttering sound, like a big kite in the wind. It billows as though it is about to burst. The ropes which hold the sail in place are straining. Suddenly a part of the sail breaks free. It is flapping violently in the wind and the boat begins to rapidly change direction. It is floating parallel to the giant waves that are more than four metres tall. The waves rush towards the dinghy. Baath orders Himanshu to grab the sail and after a few attempts Himanshu succeeds in getting hold of it. Baath helps him tie the sail down again. Soon it begins to rain. They begin to fill the empty water bottle Camille has used the previous night. Baath says as long as it rains they can drink all the water they want.

The day passes quickly enough. They are all doing something or the other. Either bailing water from the boat, keeping the sail aloft, catching water in the tarpaulin. The ropes that hold the sail break often in the high wind and it is all they can do to keep the sail in place. The ropes are very thin, about five or six millimetres thick. Some of the ropes come apart when it squalls again. It is tough work holding the rope and tying the sail back on.

Bruno and Camille share the last banana. It has turned almost brown, but they wolf it down and keep the peel aside in the carry bag. Rama Rao resentfully watches them.

The rope breaks again. Rama Rao Sr gives the tiller to Rama Rao Jr and comes rushing up to help with getting the sail under control. He trips on the ladder and falls down. He starts cursing in Bengali and then he tells Baath in Hindi, *Yeh salah bahuth beech mein aaa raha hai saab. Mai to tang aa gaya hoon. Baar baar kyon beech mein aa raha hai?* I am going to throw this away. It is useless and I am fed up of it getting in the way.

Baath senses that Rama Rao Sr will get even more worked up if the ladder kept getting in his way. He tells Rama Rao to throw it in the sea if he wishes.

No problem. *Phek do samundar mein.*

Rama Rao picks up the ladder with both his hands and lifts it. The ladder is almost as big as him. He looks a little ludicrous as he heaves the ladder into the sea. The minute it hits the water the ladder disappears from view. Rama Rao then turns around and glares at Bruno.

In the night the waves get bigger, about five metres, Rama Rao estimates. They look frightening as they rise high above the dinghy. That night a giant wave swamps the boat when they are asleep. The wave comes in from the back with a whoosh as the dinghy rolls in the swells. It carries Camille, who wakes up screaming, and Bruno down to the floorboards .

Himanshu, who is lying on the floorboards when Camille and Bruno fall on him, fears that the next wave will be big enough to break the dinghy in two. There is much sea water sloshing around the boat. They are more than ankle deep in it. They begin to bail out the sea water as fast as they can with whatever they can get hold of. After that nobody can go back to sleep. As the night progresses the waves gradually become smaller. It is a sign that the sea is calming down. The wind begins to lose its power too. Towards dawn they can see tiny patches of sky between the clouds. The clouds become fewer.

At the dawn of the fourth day the air is very still. By early morning the sea has become flat. It gleams like an endless mirror. The sun comes up and burns through the clouds and it is miserably hot. It is only five in the morning by their watch. Then it strikes them since they are travelling east it must be later than five. Maybe six thirty or seven. The boat is not moving; the sail hangs limp. Everything is still. There is not a ripple in the sea. The dinghy is utterly still. There is no sound at all, not even the sound of the smallest wavelet lapping against the dinghy because the sea is as flat as a vast swimming pool. It is so bright they have to shield their eyes. Their skin begins to burn. Camille jumps into the sea, happy the storm has passed. She swims all around the dinghy. Ten minutes later she comes back on the boat. Without the ladder she has to clamber on to the metal framework that holds the rudder, clasp the side of the dinghy and lift herself up. Baath gives her a hand and helps her into the dinghy. Baath can see she is feeling much better. For the first time in three days Camille smiles. She begins to talk to Baath a little.

By eight in the morning the sea becomes a deep blue. The sun continues to beat mercilessly down on them. There is nothing in sight except the sea, stretching endlessly in every direction. There is not the smallest wisp of cloud in the sky. By eleven whatever joy had been there after the storm passed has evaporated. It is miserable. They are all sweating, asking for more water. Rama Rao Jr looks listless. He seems to be thirstier than the rest, always asking for water.

Kya ho gaya tumko Ramiah, asks Baath. What has happened to you Ramiah?

Kuch nahin sahib. Bus pyas lagi hai, Rama Rao Jr responds. Nothing sir, just thirsty.

Sukka phek do pyas bandh ho jayegi, Baath says. Spit out whatever it is that you are chewing.

Phekne ke liye kuch raha nahin sahib, Rama Rao Jr says. There is nothing left to spit. He looks miserable.

Baath says, Look here this water has to last us till god knows when. We do not know when it will rain again. So I am going to ration the water out.

With the bottom half of the mineral water bottle that had been cut, Baath rations out the water. 150 ml to each. One by one they take turns to drink it. First Camille, then Bruno, and so on. Baath drinks the last. An hour later they ask for more water.

Let's take down the sail and put it back on the frame, Baath says. There is no wind anyway and we are going nowhere. If we take the sail down we will have some shade. We will sweat less. They take down the sail and put the tarpaulin back on. They erect the second tarpaulin in the back of the boat for the two Rama Raos to shelter from the sun. As they sit in the shade, they realize even this is not much help against the heat. Baath doles out another round of water. Himanshu looks around for something he can store his portion of the water in. In the corner near the engine he discovers a small mineral water bottle, one that holds about 250 ml. He asks Baath to pour his share into that. Baath obliges. Himanshu pours the water into his mouth, swirls it around for a while, wetting the insides of his mouth, trying not to drink it, and spits what remains back into the bottle. He closes the bottle and puts it away. Baath takes stock of the water situation. More than half of the first bottle of the mineral water is now gone.

If we are going to drink water at this rate, we are not going to last very long, Baath tells Bruno and Camille.

So what do you propose now? asks Bruno.

We should get into the water, suggests Baath. We should all be in the water. We will be cooler then. We can come back into the boat only in the evening when the sun is going down. That way we will save water and live longer.

How will we stay in the water? asks Bruno. We can't stay in there for hours, can we?

Of course we can, says Baath.

How?

We can tie a rope on both sides of the dinghy and we can hold on to the rope. If we are immersed in the sea we'll be cooler. We will not sweat so much and therefore we will not feel thirsty so often.

If you are going to be in the water, there is going to be reverse osmosis. Your body is going to lose more fluids than it would if you are in the boat in the shade.

I think it is the other way around my friend. If you sit on the boat and sweat profusely you are going to lose more body fluids than if you are in the water where it is cooler. Reverse osmosis or no reverse osmosis I am going to get into the water. What about you Camille?

Camille says in English, I think Baath is right. We should be in the water. It is nice down there. It is cooler.

Baath turns around, looks at Rama Rao and Himanshu and asks them. Himanshu looks uneasy. Rama Rao Jr is sprawled near the bow. He is not moving. He appears to be sleeping. Rama Rao Sr keeps quiet.

He thinks of how Goriah, Rama Rao's relative had got bitten in the water not once but twice and in the same area. The first time when Goriah and his brother had put out nets for fishing off Ross Island, not in deep waters but in two or three metres of water. Usually they left the nets untouched for two or three hours and then went and pulled it out of the water along with the fish caught in it. A portion of the net had got caught in a rock and Goriah had dived in to free the net. Unfortunately right under the rock where the net had got caught there was a banded sea snake. These snakes are either white and black or light yellow and black or dark blue and black, all very poisonous. The females grow up to two metres while the males are not more than one and a half feet or two feet. Banded sea snakes have tiny mouths and cannot bite on large surfaces. They go for the nose or the earlobe or the fingertip. Goriah was bitten on his little toe.

He felt the sharp pain stabbing him and saw the snake as well. Immediately Goriah headed for the surface because he knew the snake was ten times more poisonous than any land snake. He told his brother, who was on the dinghy, what had happened. His brother took the dinghy straight to Aberdeen Jetty across the water from Ross Island and took him to the main road. Goriah was quite conscious as he hurried along without a problem. As it happened there was an autorickshaw right there at the jetty and within minutes he was in the emergency ward of GB Pant Hospital. The doctors told Goriah's brother that had he come ten minutes later he would have been dead. For months afterwards Goriah's leg remained swollen. They gave him very high dosages of antibiotics. For the next six months he couldn't go fishing. Even now, years afterwards, the leg on which he was bitten is thicker and bigger than the other leg.

About nine months after the snake bite, Goriah was back

in the same area of Ross Island, diving to retrieve something that had fallen off the dinghy when a curious moray eel came swimming around him. It came from behind and Goriah saw it from the corner of his eye. He turned around and the eel went around his neck again and circled towards his back. It was not far from him. Goriah thought he should catch the eel by its neck before it bit him. He quickly lunged his hand out to catch it and the moray eel bit him, its mouth clamped on his forearm. It wouldn't let go. Goriah could not shake the eel off, no matter how hard he struggled. He did not know what to do. His hand was hurting unbearably and he saw small clouds of his blood billowing in the sea water. His lungs were beginning to ache from holding his breath. Finally he caught the neck of the moray eel with his free hand and swam to the surface with the eel still struggling in his free hand, its mouth clamped firmly to the other arm. In the dinghy they could make out there was a commotion under water and they were peering into the sea. Goriah surfaced near the dinghy, screaming in pain, the moray eel writhing and thrashing about in the water, not letting go of his hand. They tried pulling him into the dinghy. When they couldn't, one of them jumped into the sea with a *dao* and, while Goriah held on with one hand to the dinghy, held the moray eel's long, slithering body, cut its neck and threw the body into the sea. Only after that did the grip loosen and they managed to prise the head from Goriah's profusely bleeding hand. The head was almost as big as a football and its eyes still staring as he threw it back into the sea. Goriah was rushed to the hospital. It required twenty two stitches on his hand to fix it. Here in the unfathomable depths, Rama Rao wonders what creatures swim underneath them. He is mortally afraid of sharks, *badmash machchi*.

Sir, it is very deep over here, says Himanshu. We do not know the waters. Should we risk it? We might drown.

Nonsense. We have enough life jackets here. You can put them on. Take them out.

Sir, what if there are crocodiles in the water? Himanshu looks worried.

Crocodiles? Here? In the open sea? Are you out of your mind? You have seen crocodiles in Chidiyatapoo when we go out sometimes haven't you?

Yes sir.

Crocodiles stick to familiar places. They hunt near the shore. They don't come out into the open sea.

What are you two arguing about, asks Bruno.

Himanshu is afraid of crocs in the water, says Baath. I am telling him crocodiles don't come out this far into the open sea.

Hah! Bruno exclaims, of course they do! In Australia there have been instances of salt water crocodiles which have been radio-tagged, swimming over 200 miles, using ocean currents migrating from one part of the world to another. They can swim for days without food.

We are not in Australia, Baath points out. And here all the recorded instances of crocodiles killing humans have been in the mangrove creeks or mouths of the creeks, not in the open sea.

I heard in the hotel in Port Blair that there was an attack of an American tourist in one of islands near where we were diving, an area where no crocodiles were supposed to be, Bruno says.

Again, that happened near the shore, at Neil's Cove, at Havelock. Not in the open sea, Baath points out.

Bruno is quiet. Then Baath says, I was there coincidentally

the next morning, I can assure you that it was not in the open sea. But yes, that area had no previous record of crocodile sightings.

Baath tells Himanshu to pull out the life jackets. Himanshu reluctantly pulls out the life jackets. There are four of them, thermocol life jackets.

Himanshu, do you know how to swim? Baath asks.

Yes sir I know.

How long have you known how to swim?

Since I was a baby, sir. My father taught me how to swim when I was a baby.

So why are you worried now?

I don't know sir.

You wear this life jacket. Nothing will happen. *Kuch nahin hoga. Utro paani mein*. You won't even have to swim. These are thermocol life jackets. These float forever. You know when I joined the merchant navy they used to give us inflatable life jackets. The ones filled with air.

I know sir, I have seen one in a flight to Calcutta when I took my father for an operation. The air hostess showed us how to work it.

That life jacket you saw was a useless one, Himanshu. This is the real life jacket. The navy discontinued it. Do you know why?

No sir.

They discontinued it because you never know when the air will escape or when it will spring a leak or get punctured. There is no guarantee that the air will stay in it. They can leak even due to a faulty valve. But if you wear this you don't have to worry at all. They have thermocol in the front, back and in the neck. You will float forever.

Baath hands out one to Himanshu, one to Camille, one to Rama Rao Sr. Rama Rao Jr still lies sprawled in the same position. Baath tells Rama Rao Sr, Go give this to him, wake him up.

We can wear the buoyancy jackets, Baath tells Bruno. Bruno doesn't say anything. Baath gives him a buoyancy jacket and gets into the sea and asks Rama Rao Sr to hand him the rope. Baath ties the rope all along one side of the dinghy, the same way it is in lifeboats. First he ties the rope on one side, loops it through the gaps along the prow, and then does the same on the other side. At the end of it there is still enough rope on both sides for them to hold and stay in the water. Baath tests the rope to see if it is tied properly.

Camille wears her life jacket and enters the sea. Nobody else wants to come in.

Himanshu, *aa jao*, says Baath. *Dekho kuch nahin hoga*, Look nothing will happen. Himanshu reluctantly comes into the water as well. For a while he is scared. He keeps looking around then he holds the rope and floats. Rama Rao Sr comes in next. Only Bruno and Rama Rao Jr are in the boat. Bruno is sweating heavily. There is no sign of Rama Rao Jr.

Rama Rao, *Zara dekho to usko kya ho gaya hai*, Baath says Find out what has happened to him.

Rama Rao climbs on to the boat and goes across to the bow of the dinghy where Rama Rao Jr lies still on the plank. He is covered in a film of sweat. He appears to be sleeping. The sun is beating down on him, and Rama Rao Jr is oblivious.

Sahib yeh to so raha hai. He is sleeping.

Jagao usko. Wake him up.

Rama Rao tries to wake him up. He doesn't move. Rama Rao lies along the bow, reaches into the sea, scoops some water into his palm and sprinkles it on Rama Rao Jr's face. He still doesn't move.

Yeh to hil nahin raha hai sahib, Rama Rao Sr shouts. The man is not moving.

Yeh sab sukka ka kamal hai, says Baath. He tells Camille, you know he chews this *sukka*, this thing that is like a tobacco leaf. He keeps chewing on it and gets high. Now that he has run out of it, he is having withdrawal symptoms.

Do you have any medicine for this? asks Camille.

I have a very good medicine for this. Himanshu, Baath says, go into the boat, help Rama Rao put the life jacket on Ramiah and then throw him into the sea.

Himanshu looks puzzled. Sir, throw him into the sea?

Yes, throw him into the sea. He will be all right once he is in the water.

Himanshu gets on to the boat and lifts Rama Rao Jr to a sitting position while Rama Rao Sr puts the life jacket over his head and fixes the clasps so it stays in place. Rama Rao Jr does not move. Both Himanshu and Rama Rao Sr look at Baath uncertainly.

What are you waiting for? Throw him into the sea. Now, orders Baath.

Himanshu and Rama Rao lift Rama Rao Jr and slide him feet first into the water. The dinghy rocks as the balance tilts to one side. Bruno moves to the other side to keep the balance.

Rama Rao Jr is now in the water. His eyes are open. He looks around and frantically begins to swim. Baath says, *Ab jaag gaye kya? Bola na sukka math khao.*

Both Himanshu and Rama Rao Sr are laughing, as is Camille. That is good medicine, she says, where did you learn this?

In the navy they teach you everything, says Baath.

He looks at Bruno. Bruno is the only one who is not smiling.

Camille calls to Bruno and asks him to stop being difficult and come into the water. She speaks in English.

Bruno also replies in English.

What if the boat moves? Somebody has to be in it to control it.

Don't worry about it, says Baath. Since we will be holding on to the rope we will move with the boat. In any case, there is no current here and now.

Reluctantly Bruno wears the buoyancy jacket and joins them. He holds on to the rope silently.

The sea is blue and transparent. Himanshu can see the sunlight go down into the depths and turn a dark blue. He can see into the water. He knows it is more than three thousand feet of water between him and the black bottom of the sea. He tries desperately not to think of what lurks under the water, in those terrible depths.

Mona Lisa Baath

Mona Lisa Roy met Baath while she was studying commerce at Shreemati Nathibai Damodar Thackeray Women's University in Mumbai. She was the youngest of three children. She was born in Calcutta but her father who had been in the Navy had moved back to Bombay when she was a year old. Avtaar Singh Baath was stationed at Okha, in Gujarat, when Mona first met him. He had come to Bombay for the weekend before he was to go to the National Defence Academy at Khadakvasla where he had studied. He met Mona through some of her friends whom he knew. Mona who had been on her way to college, impulsively took him home instead. That day she didn't attend college. In the evening they went out. This was in 1984.

She next saw him eight or nine months later, again by accident. Mona was walking to her college when she thought she recognized a lean, tall, muscular sardar in a *pagdi* (turban) playing cricket in the *maidan*, an open patch of land where boys played hockey or cricket. Baath was fielding in a corner when she went over to him and asked him what he was doing there. He told her he was now aboard a ship and it had stopped over at Bombay because someone was getting married.

Three and a half years after they first met, Baath got his mother over to Mona's house to meet her parents. Mona's parents got along with Baath and were very fond of him. Baath's mother wanted the wedding immediately. Mona was twenty, Baath almost twenty nine. Mona didn't think she was ready to lead a married life. Mona told Baath's mother she wanted to go to college and graduate before she married. So her marriage was fixed for a date after she'd graduate. On her father's birthday.

After the date had been decided upon, Mona saw an advertisement calling for flight stewardesses for Gulf Air. They had called for graduates and she was not one yet. She was in her second year in the college and had one more year to go before she completed the course. But her sister, Shobori, an air hostess herself, encouraged her saying that it would be a good experience to attend the interview. Mona quite liked the idea.

When Shobori had joined Panam three years ago in 1986 it had been Mona who had pushed her to apply. You would be crazy not to apply. It is glamorous. It will be exciting. You will see places. What is the worst that can happen? You might get rejected. Big deal! You will be mad not to go ahead.

Mona had egged her sister on. Shobori got the job and now she was based in Bombay, so she didn't leave home. Mona applied for the position, thinking, she didn't stand to lose anything. To her surprise she did her interview well. She was told she could join Gulf Air right away or apply again after she finished college. Mona said she was fine with joining without graduating.

As she walked out of the interview room Mona felt elated. The job was perfect. The money was good. She really liked the idea of travelling. Her mother was not very happy when she came home and broke the news. I thought you wanted to study, she chided Mona. But Mona was very excited and she wanted the job.

Mona was the first of her siblings to leave home. She hadn't told her employers that she was betrothed to be married and would work only for a year. In that brief year Mona wanted to travel to all the destinations Gulf Air went to. In 1988, the airline flew to Abu Dhabi, Oman, Sharjah, Muscat, Kuwait. She went to Jordan once but did not get off the aircraft since the schedule was only to touch down and fly out. She went to Egypt, Nairobi, Dar es Salaam, London, Bangkok – which had all been exotic names in the map until then, places she never dreamed of visiting.

She had been based in Bahrain where Gulf Air had a lot of air hostesses living.

Less than a year into the job Mona was counting the days that were left before she would get married. She couldn't wait to leave. She couldn't wait to see Baath again. Sometimes she flew down from Bahrain to Bombay just to see him and Baath would come to Bombay from Cochin or Vizag, where he was posted and attached to a ship. They wrote long, tender letters to each other. There was a pigeon hole where the airlines stored her post for her. When she got back after a four day schedule Mona would find four letters from Baath in her pigeon hole. Baath wrote to her each day they spent away from each other. There would be a letter for each day. They finally got married on March 9, 1989. It was the best day of their life. The next day Mona and Baath were to go to Chandigarh and perform the *akhand path*, a Sikh marriage ceremony. For two days continuously the Guru Granth Sahib was to be read out in a gurudwara. But that part of her wedding never happened.

The day they got married, Baath received two telegrams from his unit. The first congratulated him on his wedding. The second recalled him for duty immediately. His ship was moving to Trincomalee in Sri Lanka for peace keeping duties. It was sailing the next day.

* * *

There is a picture of Mona sitting in a bullock cart wearing a brown salwar kameez. The cart is going along a mud track and green fields stretch all around to the edge of the frame. In the picture you cannot see Mona's face because it is covered by a yellow dupatta. Mona was not the kind to cover her face, although she did wear a gauze-like veil which was part of her uniform while she was a stewardess. There is a black and white picture of her wearing the uniform with the veil. It sits in the corner of her drawing room in her Port Blair house, on a mantle next to a picture of Baath, also black and white, wearing his Navy whites. In the picture he wears a turban. His hair was longer than Mona's back then. He cut it short years later at Wellington Island, Kochi, but kept a straggly beard. If someone had told Mona that once she married Baath she would have to wear a veil, she would have laughed it off. Nothing had prepared Mona for life in Baath's village, Bohli, where she spent some weeks after marriage. It was near Panipat, in Haryana. Baath had a big family there: uncles, their sons, their sons' sons, all sardars. The village was a far cry from Bombay's fashionable Colaba where Mona had grown up. In Bholi, Mona felt like an outsider. She got used to covering her head because there was no privacy in the village. If she was sleeping in the room she would cover her head because anyone could come into the room unless it happened to be latched from the inside. There were latches on the doors but nobody used them. So every time anyone came into the room, especially if it was a male cousin of Baath, Mona would automatically reach for the dupatta to cover her head. It soon became second nature.

The houses in the village lay scattered. Each family had a few acres of land and the house would be in the center of it. It was a ten minute walk from one house to the next, through the fields. The cattle were kept in the residential compound. A wall separated the house from the cattle. The buffaloes and the cattle attracted flies which swarmed all around the house. It was like living in a fish market. A strong smell of dung hung in the air like a thick, physical pall. It took Mona many days to learn to ignore the smells which she felt followed her everywhere.

There were no toilets in the village. The villagers went out to the field to answer the call of nature. The women went first. They set out very early in the morning while the stars were still in the sky. They squatted in the field and chatted while they relieved themselves. The men went separately. Mona naturally found it uncomfortable. In the beginning a couple of times she went with her mother-in-law but it was too embarrassing. She preferred to go when Baath went but in the village it was simply not done. But she insisted she would go only with Baath. The first time they went together, as they reached the fields, Mona told Baath that he should go to one corner of the field while she would find a place in the other corner. As Baath was half way Mona suddenly remembered something she had wanted to tell him and called out his name. All at once three or four heads of sardars popped up from the fields to look enquiringly at Mona. Mona had never been so embarrassed. She tried to duck and hide. But Baath came back all the way enquiring loudly what was wrong.

The women in the village gawked at Mona as though she were an alien. She felt a strong resentment from the womenfolk because Baath had married outside his community and there was a curiosity about what kind of woman he had found for himself. Baath may have trampled upon the hopes of some village girl, Mona thought. Every small gesture came in for scrutiny and invited barbed comments. Mona didn't respond to those comments. She pretended as though she didn't understand Punjabi well enough.

A couple of days after she came to Bholi, Mona was informed that the village women wanted to meet her. She had been apprehensive when she was led to a large room full of women. They were either sitting on charpoys or on the floor or were standing. They were all talking loudly but the minute Mona entered the room there was silence. No one spoke. They kept staring silently at Mona, all of them. It was as if a switch had been turned off. Mona felt spooked. She felt as though she was at an inquisition. Mona was aware that no one in the village had married an outsider but here was a wall of silence towering over her. Mona knew that wall had to be broken down. She waited for someone to say something, ask something. Nobody spoke. The silence was oppressive. At last Mona looked at one of the women and asked her a question in Hindi. She got a hesitant response in Punjabi. Soon she was asking everybody questions and getting more responses. She told them a little about herself and then it was time to eat dinner.

The men went out early in the morning to work and came back only in the evening. The conditions were very basic. Electricity would go off often. When the men came back and freshened up before dinner, they would sit around in charpoys drinking. Whatever was cooked, the vegetable or meat would be passed around for the men to have with their drinks. Once after dinner, Baath, who was sitting with his cousins and uncles, said to his oldest uncle, You know, Mona knows a Punjabi song! Mona was embarrassed. There was music in Mona's family. Her brother taught classical music. Mona sang well, too. Whenever anybody came to her house Mona's mother would make her sing. She hated that. Her mother appointed a guruji as well to teach her music. Whenever the guruji would come in through the front door Mona ran out of the back door. She didn't want to be pinned down to singing lessons. Don't make me sing in front of others and I will learn, she kept telling her mother. Mona's mother wouldn't agree.

When Baath's uncle asked her to sing in front of all the relatives, Mona couldn't say no. Everybody looked expectantly at her. Mona was relieved that it was dark. She counted time by snapping her finger and began singing '*Charkha Mera Rangla*'. Her voice rose clear into the night sky without hesitation and began to soar with the tune. Soon Baath began to clap to her singing and others joined in as well. By the time her song was over, everybody had begun to clap and they rushed forward to give her money. Baath's oldest uncle said: 'Our own girls can't sing like that!' For the first time Mona regretted that she had not learnt to sing formally.

* * *

It was September, and the evenings were pleasant. One night Mona and Baath decided to sleep on the roof. The only way up was a rickety wooden ladder that leaned against the side of the house with a step missing. There were a couple of charpoys on the roof, narrow beds with wooden frame and ropes woven taut into it. They carried some blankets to cover themselves. Sleeping on the charpoy was like settling into a hammock. It was cool in the night and the sky was full of stars with only a few clouds. For a long time Mona stared at the stars in the night sky, the skies she had flown as a stewardess. It all seemed so very long ago. She covered her head with the blanket to shut off the whining of the mosquitoes. The only other sound from the surrounding fields were the frogs croaking and the chirping of crickets. In the middle of the night Mona was shaken awake. It had begun raining and they had to get down in a hurry. Mona went down first, clutching her blanket preciously. The ladder was already slippery with rain. Mona remembered that one broken step of the ladder and carefully lowered herself, step by step, the ladder shaking gently, the rain falling on her all the while. Baath had to wait for her to get to the ground because he feared the ladder wouldn't take their combined weight. Then it was Baath's turn to come down. He came down hurriedly and missed his footing on the missing step, lost his balance and slipped down the ladder, holding his blanket. Under his weight the rung below the missing one gave way and broke with a loud crack that could be heard above the sound of the rain. He fell down to the ground with a thud and the ladder swayed and fell on top of him. There were bruises on his legs and back. The next day Baath came down with a fever which lasted two full days.

There was always a good breeze, the living room was large and airy and extended in an L-shape into the dining area. A large balcony abutted the living area. Mona filled the balcony with exotic plants she collected. Both of her sons, Karan and Aman loved running around the house or racing up the driveway on their bicycles.

Baath had received about eleven lakh rupees in gratuity, seed money to start afresh. He began to look around for a boat to buy. Soon he found one. It didn't have a name and neither had its owner bothered to list it. It was about thirty feet long and ran on a diesel engine. Baath paid three and a half lakh rupees for it. The boat's engine was on its last legs so he got the engine replaced along with some new chairs and seats. Baath sought permission from the forest department to run the boat between Wandoor, near Chidiyatapu and some nearby islands. During his service years he had made many trips to Jolly Buoy and Red Skin Islands where there were many private boats plying. Because of his Navy background, the forest department gave him permission to run the boat to Red Skin, Jolly Buoy as well as Cinq Islands. Not many were given the permit to make the run up to Cinq Islands in the Mahatma Gandhi Marine National Park. Cinq lay about twelve nautical miles from Chidiyatapoo, the southernmost part of South Andaman.

The first booking Baath got was from Port Blair to Cinq Islands, two small uninhabited islands connected by a sand bar. From Port Blair it was 20 nautical miles away. Fifteen tourists signed on and Baath went along too. They took a dinghy with them. The boat could not get onto Cinq Island directly. It had to be anchored a little off the island and the passengers had to be transferred to the dinghy which would then head for the beach. The beach in Cinq Island is beautiful. This was Baath's second

Island Hopping

On July 1, 2000, the day Commander Avtar Singh Baatl spent twenty years in the Indian Navy he decided that l longer wanted to continue there. Mona supported this deci The next question was where should they go to live once retired? Baath's house was in Mohali, Punjab. His mother his brother lived there now. Although a Bengali, Mona lived most of her life in Bombay. She did not know Pun She didn't have friends in Mohali and was not keen on goir live the rest of her life there. She had no idea what she woul there when Baath was away sailing. So Mohali was ruled ou they settled in Bombay they would have to find a house in suburbs. Mona's mother's house was in Malad. Her brother elder sister also lived in Bombay. But Bombay was too expens a proposition, and Baath didn't really relish the idea of Boml commutes. Baath and Mona decided that they would stay on Port Blair after retirement.

Three months later, Baath left the Navy on September 2000. By December that year they had found a house they bo liked and wanted to live in in Sahajeevan Nagar at Haddows. was a two bedroom apartment on the first floor of a two stor structure that perched on the hillside overlooking Haddo jetty. Above, on the hill over the colony was the Port Blair zo visit to the island. The sea around the island is clear and the sand so white it hurts your eyes on a sunny day. There is quite a bit of coral off the northern beach. It is heaven for snorkellers and divers. After the trip Baath disembarked the tourists at Chidiyatapoo and proceeded to Wandoor where the boat would be parked. Mona and Baath got 2100 rupees for the trip, their first earning.

Baath loved fishing. His friend Captain Ashwini Kumar, who was at the Naval headquarters in Port Blair, found a fisherman called Goriah and his brother, Rama Rao, who had a small dinghy. Baath and Ashwini Kumar began to go fishing in that dinghy and were soon hooked. They caught fish with the line Goriah gave them. They fished every weekend. After Ashwini Kumar was transferred as the Harbour Master for Port Blair, Admiral Harinder Singh also came on some of the fishing trips. They took the admiral fishing in an inflatable rubber dinghy with an outboard engine. Sensing their keenness for fishing the admiral gifted them a Burmese dinghy which had been captured from poachers.

The dinghy had been lying idle with the navy for a long time. It was longer than the boat Baath had bought. It was thirty-five feet long, five feet longer. At its widest, it was narrower than the boat, about seven feet. It had a seven horse power Chinese engine which began to give problems and they had trouble finding spares. Baath found a second hand eight horse power Kirloskar engine and installed it in the dinghy alongside the Chinese engine and began using it for their fishing trips. Ashwini Kumar's cargo manager Jagdish Rao, also a keen fisherman, joined the two and the three would go fishing every weekend on the dinghy. Jagdish arranged the food for the trips while one of the others brought along the drink, usually a bottle of rum. They would set out at four in the evening and come back at ten in the night. Often they would come back much later as well, at midnight. If the fishing was really good they got back only the following morning at four. They loved to fish in the night. Many fish bit only in the night.

Goriah and Rama Rao were made in charge of running the dinghy. When Baath or Ashwini Kumar were not fishing they were free to use the dinghy to fish. And whenever Baath wanted to go fishing Rama Rao had to take them. After three months Baath bought a second eight horse power Kirloskar engine and removed the Chinese engine altogether.

For about seven months after he left the Navy, Baath did not work. He bought four diving tanks from a man who taught diving but was moving on to South Africa. He got a couple of regulators, fins and buoyancy jackets. Mona was fond of diving, having done her first dive during a trip to Mexico. Baath was a qualified Navy diver. He had done a one year clearance diving officers course. In the morning, Mona and Baath and the children began to go to North Bay in the dinghy to snorkel and dive. Then they would go to Madhuban and eat lunch on the beach. In the afternoons they went fishing. Sometimes they brought the fish they caught back home. Sometimes they took it to a hotel and had it cooked there. At other times Baath took the fish they caught to the Naval Officer's Institute near his house and had the fish served to everybody else there as well.

Mona and Baath decided to organize a camp and take the children along too. Ashwini Kumar's two daughters were sixteen and eighteen years old; he also had a nephew living with him who was fifteen. Karan was eight and Aman, five. They planned to take the dinghy out for five days. Baath had an icebox made on the dinghy with planks lined with thermocol and polythene so they could store cold water, beer, cold drinks, and some chicken and fish in it. Ashwini Kumar made a small box which had twenty compartments. These compartments would store various spices: turmeric, salt, chilly powder, coriander powder, bay leaf, cloves, nutmeg, whatever was needed to cook. They planned to set off for Rutland Island which is across the waters from Chidiyatapoo, Sisters Island, Cinq and North Brother. They decided to take Goriah and Rama Rao as well as Goriah's dinghy, as back up. Baath asked the dinghy to reach Chidiyatapoo at six one morning and they set off soon afterwards.

The first stop was a beach in Rutland Island, seven miles away. There was a fishing village nearby but they stayed away from it. Baath and Ashwini showed the children how to pitch the tents and assigned them the task of pitching tents for the rest of the trip. The children were also tasked with collecting firewood for the cooking. They had taken a couple of spatulas, a frying pan, a large wok and a grill for barbeque. Breakfast was their first meal. They fashioned a stove out of Kewda wood from the trees that grew along the shore because it doesn't burn easily. Once they made a stove out of Kewda branches, they placed firewood under it, put a grill on top and made omelettes which they ate with bread for breakfast. The children went off for a swim while the women made lunch: rice, chicken, and vegetables for Mrs Kumar who did not eat meat. Ashwini Kumar took out chilled beer from the icebox. The dinghy carried five jerry cans of water; each could hold 35 litres. The count was one can a day. The water was for drinking, cooking, brushing teeth only. Nobody was to waste water.

After a relaxed lunch washed down with beer the men set out fishing off Rutland Island. In about half an hour they caught about six kg of fish, a Kukari which weighed about three kilos and some smaller fish: a grouper and a couple of coral fish. Goriah and Rama Rao cleaned the fish and prepared them for the barbeque. In the evening they made a huge bonfire by the beach and drank rum and sang Hindi film songs that everybody joined in. After dinner while the women and the girls went into the tents to sleep, the boys and the men spread a tarpaulin on the beach, next to the bonfire, and slept under the stars. The bonfire kept the crabs and centipedes away. They were dead tired and slept straight through the night. While they slept, Goriah and Rama Rao Sr, who had their own icebox in their dinghy, went out to fish.

Early in the morning Baath woke everybody up; they rolled up the tents, ate breakfast, and set off for Sisters Island sixteen miles south of Cinq. Sisters also had a sand bar, though narrower than the one in Cinq. The waves from both sides of the sand bar crashed high and it was possible to walk right through the crashing waves to the other part of the island. They found that on the western part of the island the sand was white and full of small white shells. On the other side the sand was black. They stayed away from the black beach. Children collected shells. There were not many trees near the beach but it was not too hot. They swam, snorkelled, and had lunch by the beach. In the afternoon without warning it began to rain heavily so they showered in the rain which stopped as abruptly as it had begun. They headed back to the sea again, this time to fish.

In the evening they lit another bonfire by using the logs that had washed up on the beach. One log was hollow. Ashwini Kumar and his nephew Gopal held one end of it and Baath lifted the other end. This log had been half eaten by the waves and had innumerable tiny holes in it, probably bored by insects.

They placed it at the edge of the bonfire so they could feed the fire when it was dying down. Gopal sat on the far end of the log. In the heat of the fire, all the ants in it swarmed towards the end Gopal was sitting on and began to bite him. Gopal ran straight into the sea and plunged in and stayed there for some time to escape the fury of the ants. For a long time afterwards he couldn't sit down without wincing in pain.

The next day as they were leaving the sea became choppy. The plan was to go to North Brother and from there to South Cinq Island. In the choppy sea it would be difficult to get to North Brother so they headed for Cinq, which was only five miles away. If the weather permitted they would proceed to North Brother afterwards. At South Cinq the gradient of the beach is very steep. It starts to fall right at the beach. As a result when the tide comes in the big waves crash right on the beach. When the dinghy approached the shore with the big waves behind it there was every chance of it getting swamped. Luckily that morning it was low tide. They made the landing without much trouble. The beach was already hot. It stretched for about two hundred metres before the tree line began. They got their provisions and tenting materials off the boat and made it to the tree line through the scorching sand. It was so hot that nobody felt like walking across the sand again to get to the sea for a swim. Rama Rao Sr climbed a coconut tree and threw some coconuts down so everybody had tender coconut water to drink. They didn't go fishing in the afternoon because the waves were very big and the dinghies were anchored beyond the swells that rushed up to the beach.

By evening the spot they had chosen to camp swarmed with mosquitoes and sand flies. To ward off the insects Baath had brought along an insect repellent the army used while on jungle counter insurgency operations. It was called Dap. It was very smelly and had to be smeared all over the exposed body parts. But the insects stayed away from it. The next morning when they were about to leave, the tide had come in. Huge waves were crashing on the beach. Goriah and Rama Rao both said that they had roughly thirty seconds to get into the dinghy. They had to get in immediately as a wave crashed and the dinghy had to be pulled out before the next one came in and broke on the beach. The dinghy would get swamped if the wave came in when the boat was still on the beach. The boat had to ride the wave and enter the sea. It was a tricky operation but everybody managed to get in. Then the second dinghy came in and the provisions were loaded in quickly and the second dinghy too rode the incoming wave and headed into the sea. Thus ended the third night. They cancelled the trip to North Brother which was 20 miles out and came back to Rutland and camped in a different spot. That was the last night and the next day they went back to Chidiyatapoo. It was as though the rest of the world hadn't existed during the time they were out island hopping.

The Fight

Badmash machchi aa jayega, Rama Ramo Sr is telling Baath. The sharks will come. He is clinging on to the rope next to Baath and looks worried.

Aa to saḳta hai. Kyon nahin aa saḳta hai? Baath responds carefully. He can see where this is going.

Of course a shark can come. Why can't it come?

Himanshu is listening to the conversation now.

Aayega toh hamein ḳha jayega, Rama Rao goes on. He thinks it is logical that if a shark swims up to them it will proceed to eat one of them.

Mujhe toh nahin lagta, says Baath confidently. I don't think it follows that if a shark comes up it will eat us.

Aa jayega sahib, Rama Rao Sr says, *Aur hamein zinda ḳha jayega*. They'll come, they'll come and eat us alive.

Mujhe nahin lagta hai ḳi aisa hoga, says Baath. He knows that being in the water for hours is making them anxious. Occasionally they go back to the boat but come back again into the water when they begin to sweat. Rama Rao went to the boat and came back. Bruno keeps going back to the boat whenever he starts getting worried about reverse osmosis.

But Rama Rao is adamant. *Hum boat mein ja rahein hain*, he

asserts and climbs on to the boat. Half an hour later, he is back in the water. He is sweating all over.

Baath climbs back on to the boat. He looks for the chewing gum he had stuck on to the side of the plank near Rama Rao. He cannot find it.

Arre mera chewing gum kahan gaya? He shouts. Where has my chewing gum gone?

Rama Rao Sr shouts back. *Hum chaba rahein hain.* I am chewing on it.

Magar woh to mera chewing gum hai! But that is my chewing gum!

Ab meri bari hai sahib. It is my turn now to chew on it. *Bhook lag rahi hai.* I am feeling hungry.

Theek hai, chabao. Magar usko math khana. Bacha ke rakhna. Okay chew it, but save it for later. Don't throw it away.

After three hours in the water, Himanshu feels thirsty. He clambers on back to the dinghy and looks for the water he has saved. He cannot find the bottle. He is puzzled. He looks around to see if it has rolled away because of the motion of the boat. Himanshu knows this is not possible since the dinghy has been still and the sea flat and calm. He thinks maybe hunger is playing tricks on his mind and that he has kept the bottle somewhere and has forgotten it. He begins to search the boat.

Baath looks at Himanshu rummaging around and asks, What has happened to you? Come down into the water.

Sir I cannot find the bottle in which I had kept my water. I am looking for it.

It will be in the boat.

Himanshu finally finds it near the tiller. It is empty. He picks it up and shakes it to see if there is any drop left. It is empty; he checks the cap, it is screwed on tight. As he looks at the empty bottle, Himanshu feels an anger rising within him.

Mera paani kisne piya? he asks loudly. Who drank my water?

Nobody replies.

What is the problem? Camille asks.

Somebody has drunk his quota of water, Baath informs her.

Humne piya, Rama Rao Jr finally says.

Kyon piya? Himanshu asks. He is furious now.

Pyas laga, pi liya, explains Rama Rao Jr. I felt thirsty, so I drank.

Magar woh pani mera tha. Maloom nahin tha kya? But that water was meant for me. Didn't you know?

Paani par naam toh nahin likha tha. The water did not have your name written on it.

Himanshu leaps into the water with a big splash and tries to punch Rama Rao Jr. His roundhouse swing misses as Rama Rao ducks and goes beneath the dinghy and swims under it to the other side. Himanshu follows and pulls Rama Rao Jr by the leg and both begin to grapple with each other in the water. Baath swiftly swims to them and tries to separate them.

I will kill you, you bloody dog, he shouts. *Maar doonga saale. Kutta saala*. Himanshu is shouting as he wrestles with Rama Rao who breaks free and quickly climbs back into the boat. Himanshu follows. Baath follows him and orders them to stop it.

Band karo yeh bakwas, Baath orders. Stop this nonsense immediately.

Why did he drink my water? He had his own water. Why did he drink my water? Himanshu's fists remain clenched.

Himanshu, listen, Himanshu listen to me, Himanshu! Baath shouts, his normally loud voice even louder. I will give you the same amount of water that you had saved. But first stop this. I will give you that water. You don't worry.

Baath pulls Himanshu to the dinghy and climbs into it. Himanshu follows, glowering at Rama Rao Jr. Baath takes the smaller bottle and pours hundred ml of water into it and gives it to Himanshu. Baath looks at Rama Rao Jr and says, Don't drink his water. This is what comes from eating sukka.

Sir, my throat was feeling dry sir, Rama Rao Jr tells Baath. That is why I drank it.

That's it. Eat more sukka. Eat more sukka, Baath mocks. Sir, I will not eat sir.

You are telling me this because your sukka is over. No sir, I will never eat sukka again, if we come out of this.

Of course we will come out and of course you will eat sukka. It will be the first thing you will do when we come out of this.

No sir, I promise.

Let's see.

Himanshu rinses his mouth with the water he has been given and carefully spits it back into the bottle. This time he keeps the bottle on the plank on which Camille sleeps. I am keeping my eye on you, Himanshu tells Rama Rao Jr, as he gets back into the sea. Everybody knows my name is written on that water. I am watching you. You drink it and you will regret it.

Don't worry Himanshu, says Baath. Don't fight. If we run out of water I will cut a portion of my thigh off for you to eat. Leg piece! I know you like leg piece! Baath is laughing now. Himanshu knows that it is forced laughter but he manages a smile.

All of them stay in the water after that. By four the sun begins to set and Baath tells everybody to get back on to the dinghy. The sky is a spectacular red. Camille points to one corner of the sky. Baath looks in the direction she is pointing. Up above, high in the sky, there are birds flying, five of them, in a V formation. They are flying too high to make out what birds they are. But everybody is happy. For the first time in four days there has been activity. They take it as a sign of hope.

It gets dark quickly. Rama Rao Sr is searching for something. He sees the paper bag in which Bruno and Camille have carefully kept the banana peels. Rama Rao puts his hand inside the bag and takes out one. It has turned black. He smells the peel and before anybody realizes it he has put it in his mouth and has eaten it. He puts his hand inside the bag to eat the second one. Camille shrieks. Baath quickly snatches at the bag in Rama Rao's hand but Rama Rao Sr is quicker. The second banana peel is in his hand and he smells it again.

Throw it away, it is rotten, says Baath. It will give you a bad stomach. You will fall sick. We do not have any medicines in the dinghy if you fall sick.

Nahin sir, yeh swadisht hai. Yeh achcha hai. Hum abhi ḳuch bhi ḳha saḳte hain. No sir, this is tasty. This is good. I can eat anything now. Even him.

Rama Rao points to Bruno Beauregard.

Chodo yeh sab baatein. Usḳo pheḳ do. Throw it away.

Sahab sab is aadmi ḳe waje se hua hai. Everything is because of this man. *Main isḳo maroonga*. I am going to kill him.

Bruno senses that something is amiss and that he is the subject of the conversation and looks at Baath as if looking for an explanation.

Baath tells Bruno, Don't worry, he is agitated because he is hungry.

Bruno shrugs his shoulders but continues to watch Rama Rao Sr warily.

Rama Rao is getting very worked up.

Main isko abhi maar dalunga. Is bhenchod ko abhi maroonga. I am going to kill this bastard right now. If it wasn't for him I'd be home now with my children and my wife.

Rama Rao is beginning to cry. He looks around for his dao.

Main isko abhi maroonga. Because of this asshole, we are all going to die at sea. Why should I die because of him? I am going to kill him first. He should die first. We would've been fine if it wasn't for him and his stupid compass. He has to die.

Baath tells Himanshu, *Uska dao pakad lo.* Himanshu grabs hold of Rama Rao who is less than half of Baath's size and sits him down on the plank and says, *Insaan hai. Galti ho gayi. Abhi usko phaasi mein chadaoge kya?*

Baath tries to reason with him. He is human. Humans make mistakes. Are you going to hang him for this? I am angry too. Very angry. I want to hit him. I want to go back home to my wife and children too. But hitting him is not going to get me home. Be sensible.

Baath takes the paper bag away from Rama Rao Sr who offers no resistance.

Arre mera chewing gum kaha rakhe ho? Rama Rao Sr says he has given it to Rama Rao Jr. Baath turns around and looks at him. In the silhouette of the setting sun, he can see that Rama Rao Jr is chewing something. His jaws are working. Baath thinks he is smiling but is not sure.

A breeze begins blowing up from the west.

Let us put up the sail again, Baath orders. Why waste the wind? At least we will move a few miles in the night.

Rama Rao Sr and Himanshu help Baath put up the sail. Bruno keeps out of Rama Rao's way. Baath gives everybody a final round of water for the day. One of the diving tanks is now empty. There are two tanks left. It is a light breeze that blows. Baath knows they will not travel far. But his greater worry is Rama Rao Sr.

Rama Rao Sr

Rama Rao Sr caught his first fish in the sea off Puri, Orissa where his father had taken him fishing. His father had only recently become a fisherman. Before that he had worked at Bengal Pottery in Calcutta. Rama Rao doesn't remember what fish it was but remembers the thrill of catching it. He had slung out a line with a live bait and after a while he'd felt the line begin to tug and pull. He shouted excitedly and began to pull the fish in. It was about two kilos and it gleamed in the sunlight, as Rama Rao pulled it into the boat. His father kept smiling as the fish flapped around on the deck of the boat trying to get back into the sea. Rama Rao let go of the line and the fish began to jump higher, its gills opening and closing. Its unblinking eyes looked accusingly at Rama Rao as it thrashed about. His father yelled at him to get a hold of the line or the fish would jump into the sea. Rama Rao's father thrust a block of wood into his hands. He can still remember the thwack thwack thwack of the wood as he clubbed the fish on the head till it became motionless and one of its eyes turned to pulp. At the end of it, he was panting with his exertions. He must have been fifteen. That afternoon the fish was cleaned and fried. As he ate the last morsels his mind was made up. He would be a fisherman, just like his father. Initially his father dissuaded him and so young Rama Rao worked in hotels as cleaner, as security guard. But he could not stick to any job. His mind was set on the sea. Three years later he succeeded in wearing his father down.

He bought a ticket to Port Blair on M V Harshavardhan from Calcutta. Bunk class. The ticket cost him exactly 101 rupees. It was a small price to pay to get to the Andamans. His relatives who occasionally visited told him colourful fishing tales. They told him that the sea around Andamans was jumping with fish. These stories cluttered Rama Rao's memories. In his imagination many of them landed right on his lap.

Ram Rao went to work for Thata Rao, related to him in some complicated way which he never managed to figure out. Everybody called Thata Rao Gabbar Singh after a villain in a Hindi film. He had a fearsome reputation and a forty-five-foot long boat with a bow that rose nine feet high above the sea, a boat in which he sailed to Andamans from Coastal Karnataka, on the west coast of India. Gabbar Singh also brought his nets from what everybody in Andamans referred to as 'mainland.' Many of Gabbar's crew came from Kakinada in Karnataka. For two years he worked on Gabbar Singh's squat boat. One of the first fish that landed in their net was an eight foot shark. They pulled the net out of the water and left it hanging above the waves for about an hour while the shark thrashed about, this way and that, trying to bite its way out of the net. When it became still they brought the shark on board and thrust iron rods into it to see if it was really dead. The shark began to wriggle this way and that, flicking its tail fin. The fin caught one of the fishermen unawares and hit him and he was knocked down with a thud. Everybody stayed clear of the shark for a while as they watched for signs of life ebbing out of it. Rama Rao remembered some of the shark stories that he had heard when he was in mainland. This shark was aggressive even out of the water. They had to attack it with daos and machetes and kill it before they cut its fins. Afterwards when they cut its belly open they found part of a plastic bucket that must have once been a bright pink, and a couple of bolts, probably part of some boat it must have tried to chew.

Sharks ate anything they bit into, anything that went into their mouth ringed with viciously sharp teeth that looked like a curved row of crooked, serrated knives. Rama Rao had once heard a story where a shark had come in from underneath and bit the thigh of a swimming fisherman, and for a few seconds the fisherman had no clue that he had been bitten by a shark. When the pain hit him, he began screaming he couldn't swim. The shark had bitten off a big piece of his thigh and by the time the other fishermen guided the dinghy where he was thrashing, the shark had turned around and was heading towards him for another bite and in the distance they could see the fins of a couple of other sharks gliding along above the small waves, converging purposefully. Rama Rao was told that sharks can smell one drop of blood in a million drops of water and can sense the struggle of a prey a mile off in the water. Here the fisherman was bleeding heavily. They managed to pull him into the dinghy just as the shark made a close pass. The boat had been ten nautical miles off the nearest island. The fisherman kept screaming in pain all the way to the shore. It was impossible to tie a rope like a tourniquet to stop the bleeding because the wound was too deep. By the time the boat reached shore the fisherman had stopped screaming altogether and had bled to death. His brother who had come fishing with him wept all the way to the hospital. When they came back to the boat from the hospital the blood had dried and flies had started coming in droves and were buzzing around. Nobody felt like cleaning the dinghy. When he saw his first shark out of the water Rama Rao realized that here was a fish he had to steer clear of. Rama Rao called sharks *badmash machchi*. The shark that he saw first, caught in the net, was a white one, a Tiger *badmash*. They had three rows of teeth zigzagging both in the upper and the lower jaws. Sharks grew 370 teeth in their lifetime. When one fell another grew in its place. The shark's mouth looked like a meat processer used for mincing meat.

Gabbar Singh's sail boat fished only for sharks. The boat would take rations for a month and set sail with eight or nine fishermen in it to catch sharks. It could hold five hundred tonnes of shark meat. Whenever they ran out of water they anchored off some island where there was water and stocked up. Whenever it rained they spread the sail out and caught water in it. The sail was made of seventy metres of cloth. To make it they stripped the kadi tree of its bark and dried the bark. Afterwards they boiled the dried bark in a huge vat of water till all the resin left the bark. In this water they soaked the sail cloth till the cloth absorbed all the resin. The resin coated the cloth in such a way that it let neither wind nor water through. The sail was now coffee brown in colour because of the resin coat. At night the fishermen slept under the sail which they stretched over the deck like a roof. The sail did not let the rain water through even if it rained all night. The provisions were kept in the back of the boat, covered with the sail cloth for protection. Three people were needed to erect the sail. They attached it to a long beam which had to be raised. The man at the tiller had the controls of the sail, in case the wind shifted abruptly, to prevent the boat from capsizing.

When the boat reached a spot where they thought there would be sharks to be caught, they let down the anchor and sank the shark nets into the sea. The nets were big, with nine-inch gaps, and stretched for four or five hundred metres across the sea with buoys on one end and weighted with stones on the other. They sank the nets in depths of thirty to seventy metres, depending on where they were fishing. The stones reached the bottom and held the net while the buoys held it from the top. A thick rope tethered the net to the sail boat. It took a long time to set the net for the sharks, and afterwards it hung like some giant spider's web, suspended seven metres below the surface of the sea reaching all the way to the sea bottom. By the time the whole net was spread it would be around four in the evening, the sun about to set. All night the net would remain in the water. While the fishermen slept, all kinds of game fish would get caught in the net: trevallies, groupers, king mackerels and yellow-fin tuna. The sharks which came to eat the fish got caught in the net and would begin to struggle and pull the net down to the bottom getting more entangled in it as they hit the bottom where their gills would soon be covered with sand and sea bottom muck. Unable to move they would choke to death, the net tightening around them.

Their work would begin early the following morning, usually by six when the sun was already up and bright. The net would be heavy with all the fish and the sharks caught in it. A good day's catch had as many as thirty sharks, some weighing more than a hundred kilos each. It took seven fishermen to slowly pull in the net. Three would stand close to the water on the boat's deck, one would stand a little behind them and three more would stand a little further apart. They began by pulling in the rope that was attached to the net. It sometimes took an entire day to pull the net in fully. Even so at sunset some of the net would still be in the water.

Most of the sharks that came up with the net would be dead by the time they were pulled in. One by one they extricated the dead sharks from the net. They began by cutting the head of the shark, hacking it off behind the eyes and before the gills began. Then they cut away the fins and kept them separately. They slit what remained of the shark lengthwise, removing the liver, the entrails and the heart and took out the rough skin. Sharks have no bones but it is still hard work to hack into the flesh. They threw the entrails into the sea. Inside the stomachs they often found other fish the shark had eaten, undigested crab shells and tortoise shells. Sometimes they found baby sharks inside pregnant sharks. They cut the rest of the shark into pieces, cleaned the pieces with sea water till all the blood left the flesh and made deep diagonal incisions into the shark meat and then salted and stored the meat in the hold with ice. Sometimes they saved the jaws and the curving serrated teeth of the bigger sharks as souvenirs to be given away. The water churned when they threw shark offal into the sea. If the net got caught in the rocks below all they could do was to cut it away. Nobody wanted to dive into the depths to retrieve the net. It was not possible to dive thirty or forty metres into the sea without oxygen tanks. Even if it were, the waters would be crazy with fish waiting to eat the fish still in the net and all the offal as well.

There was nothing they could do about the smell when they cut open the sharks. It leapt out and assailed their noses. When the smell became unbearable fishermen would take turns in going to some other part of the boat, upwind, to recover and come back to begin cutting and cleaning the shark again. The hot sun only made it worse. They would rub Amrutanjan on their nostrils when this happened, and even that didn't help keep the smell away.

Once the net was all in the boat and the sharks cut and cleaned they pulled up the anchor, unfurled the sail and set course for the next spot to spread the nets all over again. The proceeds of the sale of shark meat they divided it among themselves. First they deducted from it the cost of the rations they consumed during their voyage. Three parts of the rest went to Gabbar Singh who also owned the nets. The remainder they divided among themselves. In the early eighties the Andaman Sea had been full of sharks. There was plenty of work. For two years Rama Rao worked with Gabbar Singh and then his business sank without a trace. Rama Rao Sr went back to mainland.

His father arranged his marriage with a woman from his village. On March 15, 1986, Rama Rao Sr married Rajalamma at Wantoor. The first few years of his marriage he spent there, catching fish and tilling land. When the pull of Andamans became compelling Rama Rao and his wife set sail for Port Blair and he began to work for Gabbar Singh once again. This phase didn't last long. Rama Rao returned to the mainland but came back to Andaman soon enough. In 1991, he began to work for Subramaniam Seth to fish for sharks, this time from a dinghy, living in Mayabundar. Rajalamma's sister's husband often came with him to fish as well. They were often away from Mayabundar for days on end on fishing trips. They slept in the jungles. Sometimes his brother-in-law didn't come for the trips. He soon noticed that his brother-in-law had started staying away from the shark fishing trips more often than not. People began to tell Rama Rao that his brother-in-law had taken up with his wife. One day Rama Rao accosted his wife and this led to a flaming argument at the end of which Rama Rao forced his wife to move with him to Nimbu Thala Jetty, away from his brother-in-law's vicinity. For a couple of months they lived there together. Rama Rao continued going for the fishing trips and when he came back he kept hearing the same stories of his wife and his brother-in-law all over again. Rama Rao confronted Rajalamma again. Rama Rao remembers the date: March 22. That was the day Rajalamma hung herself after the argument. The next day, when the news reached his brother-in-law, he hung himself too. It had been a Saturday. When his brother-in-law hung himself there was no doubt in Rama Rao's mind about the liaison that had existed between them. The next day the police came and arrested Rama Rao, and took him to Mayabunder, implicating him in his wife's death. Two days later Rama Rao gave a statement stating his innocence and for three months thereafter he spent his time in Mayabundar jail. He hired a lawyer who charged him a lumpsum of 10,000 rupees to fight the case. Rama Rao Sr paid the lawyer as and when he had money to give. Some months he gave the lawyer 200 rupees, sometimes more, sometimes thousand rupees. For six years the case dragged on. In August 1997, it was dismissed for lack of evidence.

Rama Rao met Jogeswari at Anarkali Basti, near Aberdeen Bazaar in Port Blair. He was fishing with her brothers and the case was going on. Often he stayed at her house. The more he saw her the more he grew fond of her. She reciprocated. So Rama Rao Sr took her to a temple and tied a mangalsutra round her neck. They had two daughters, first Prasanti, then Kumara.

Jogeswari's elder sister had a son Ramiah, who was fifteen years younger than Rama Rao who everybody called Rama Rao Jr.

* * *

Rama Rao Sr fished throughout the year with a fishing license that allowed him to fish from Diglipur in North Andaman, which is nearly three hundred kilometres by winding roads north of Port Blair or 185 nautical miles by sea, all the way down to Hut Bay in Little Andaman, south of Rutland, beyond the Duncan Passage and the Brothers Islands. South of the Little Andaman lay the Ten Degree Channel that separated the Andaman from the Nicobar group of islands. Just south of Nicobar was the Six Degree Channel, connecting to Malacca Straits rife with pirates. It is through here the heavy traffic passed, about a 100 ships a day, oil tankers, cargo vessels, pleasure boats, and the like connecting the East to the West. Rama Rao had never gone south of Hut Bay. Beyond that the sea was unknown to him.

Normally when Rama Rao was setting off to fish the first rooster would be crowing or about to crow. Between three and four in the morning. There were usually stars in the skies when they set out. Between two and five people got into the dinghy for the journey, which would be anything between three to five days. Rama Rao's fishing mentors had told him what star would be visible at which part of the sky at what time. He read the stars to navigate. Rama Rao usually went on a hired dinghy to fish. He once had his own dinghy but it had sunk. If there were more people, four or five, they usually went on a five- or six-day trip. They loaded the boat with ice accordingly. The ice cost anything between one thousand rupees to seven thousand rupees, which was divided by five. At the end of the trip their catch was divided by five and the owner of the dinghy got a fifth of the proceeds of the fishing trip. That was his fee for hiring the dinghy. If they had to fish off Baratang they had to take five or six bars of ice. Each bar was 200 kg. There was an ice box in the dinghy where they stored the fish. They took rations: water, oil, spices for cooking, rice, vegetables, stove, utensils to prepare the dishes. They ate twice a day. There was no fixed timing. They continued to fish if the fish continued to bite. Sometimes it went on well past noon before they had their first meal of the day. At other times it was past two or three in the afternoon by the time they finished cooking. That was nearly when the day was over. The sun in this part of the world set at a quarter to five and rose at five. If they had cooked in the day they ate the leftovers in the night. If they felt like bathing they jumped into the sea. If they wanted to excrete, they squatted on the wooden beam that connected the rudder to the dinghy which was wide enough to squat on. If they wanted to urinate they went to the beam.

If the ice box was filled they would have about five or six hundred kilos of fish and they would begin the return journey. Six hundred kilos was a good catch. They sold to a wholesaler who gave them sixty rupees a kilo, irrespective of what the fish was or what size it was. Shark fins fetched a good price though, three or four thousand rupees a kilo. The wholesalers loaned Rama Rao and the other fishermen interest-free money whenever they needed. Twenty or thirty thousand rupees sometimes.

They usually fished up current. The bigger fish tend to face into the current, waiting for the current to carry the smaller fish to them. While going on the dinghy they trailed a long line to catch tuna, jackfish, kukari, surmai, dandu. Sometimes they landed big ones, twenty to twenty-five kilos in weight. They trailed lines for thirty to forty metres when the dinghy moved. At the end of the line there would be an artificial lure to bait the fish, colourful and made of rubber, with a hook inside. When the boat moved the lure made a noise while travelling through the water that attracted the fish to the lure. Fishes are sensitive and can detect vibrations, currents, and even sense the motion of other fish or the thrashing of a fish on the hook. There was an additional hundred to hundred and fifty metres of rope for the slack whenever a fish bit the lure and got hooked. Rama Rao could make out the second a fish bit the lure. He would cut the engine and slow the dinghy to give the fish some slack. The fish would begin to fight with the hook inside its mouth and the slack allowed it to swim about and tire itself out. As it tired, Rama Rao Sr pulled in the line bit by bit. When it came near the boat and started to plop out of the water Rama Rao reached out, grabbed it, and hauled it in. If it was a bigger fish he used a hook and hoisted it aboard and let it thrash around in the floorboards. Sometimes the ones that took a long time to die were thrust under the floorboard where they thudded against the floorboard till they couldn't breath anymore. Some fish fought for about an hour once they were hooked. The bigger fish sometimes took a bite out of the fish that was hooked. Once a shark took away most of a kukari that Rama Rao had caught. Rama Rao had to throw it back into the sea to use as bait.

If the fishing trip was only for a day they took cooked vegetables, rice and fried fish, headed out two and a half hours into the sea roughly 15 to 20 nautical miles and were back by three in the afternoon. They had to find the right depths to fish. Some spots were too deep, over 200 metres. Rama Rao preferred to fish in spots that were fifty to sixty metres deep, among the rocks below the sea. He carried a depth finder, a mirror tied to a piece of iron at the end of a long plastic string. Rama Rao dropped this into the water and measured the depth as the mirror sank into the water, metre by metre. The sound the mirror made when it touched the bottom told Rama Rao what kind of bottom it is, whether it was sandy or rocky. If he heard a sharp clink then the sea bottom was bound to be rocky. A sandy bottom would produce a smaller clink. The minute the boat was anchored he would know the direction the current would be flowing, the boat would begin to drift in that direction. Rama Rao also knew which direction the current would be flowing when he dropped the fishing line. Sometimes the current changed in a matter of few hours and Rama Rao had to go further and drop anchor again. He could sometimes tell what kind of fish he would get depending on the time and the spot. He marks the spots.

Rama Rao liked night fishing. At night he fished at spots where the depth was between twenty metres to fifty metres. They dropped anchor and let a couple of lines into the water. Each line had three or four hooks with live baits. They cut kaapa thane, a small fish usually about a hundred or hundred fifty grams into pieces and used them as baits on the hooks. They kept moving the lines to attract the fish. On nights when the sea was calm, they could make out the movement of the fish under them by the ripples on the surface of the sea. They could feel the fish tugging at the bait. That is when they pulled the line and the fish got hooked. Once a fish got hooked the line moved as the fish struggled and the movement attracted other fish. They caught a variety of small fish with kaapa thane as bait. Red snapper, yellow fish, butterfly fish, smaller kookari, ranvi, barracuda. Sometimes they spotted huge tortoises swimming by at nights but did not catch them. In Diglipur and Mayabunder they saw crocodiles sometimes, up the mangrove creeks, but they steered clear.

Whenever Rama Rao worked with Commander Baath he lived in the dinghy. He was the dinghy master. He looked after the equipment on the boat, ran the compressor to fill the diving tanks, steered the dinghy. His salary was 4, 000 rupees.

The Ship

You snored last night, Camille tells Baath. They are in the water. Camille is smiling at the thought of Baath snoring.

Did I? I wouldn't know if I was.

You were snoring, Camille asserts. You were snoring softly but you were definitely snoring. Softly and merrily.

Merrily?

I was wondering how you could snore like that in the middle of all this, Camille says. Her tone is accusing.

I'm really sorry if I kept you awake. But I was really tired.

I was wondering how you can sleep so soundly.

What is the point of worrying? Worrying will get us nothing.

Sir look, lots of fish here, Himanshu shouts excitedly. He is on the other side of the dinghy, holding on to the rope. He does not have as much energy to swim around as he had the day before.

All around the dinghy swarms of fish have converged. In the bright blue water they glisten like translucent gems. They are small not more than two or three centimetres in length, swarming the hull of the dinghy, swimming all round them. There are hundreds of them, maybe thousands.

Arre dekho, breakfast *aa gaya*, Baath shouts excitedly. *Itne saare machchi hai, pakkad lo jitna pakadna hai*. So many of them, grab as many as you can.

Himanshu cups his hand under one of the fish, a yellow one and closes his fist abruptly. But the fish has swum out of his grasp. Rama Rao Sr tries to catch a few but the fish dart away lightning quick. They are impossible to catch. Rama Rao Jr gets up on to the boat and comes back into the water with a large plastic bag. He is determined to trap some fish in it. He lies in wait with the bag hoping the fish will swim into it. Not a single fish comes near the bag. They swim around the bag. When he lunges with the bag towards the fish, they swim out of the way.

Bruno Beauregard is on the boat. He has found an iron rod which he keeps sharpening. He is hoping to spear a bigger fish with it, in case one comes near. Or maybe even a turtle. Turtles are slower swimmers. He peers over the hull and looks at the swarms of tiny fish and shakes his head.

Then he stands up and looks around. All he can see is the blue sea stretching to infinity. He goes back to sharpening the rod. He rubs the rod against a piece of flat iron that he has found on the boat. He feels thirsty. His saliva comes up to his mouth and he swishes it around his mouth and swallows it. Up in the air he can see birds fly. He squints into the sun to see what path they are taking, shielding his eyes with the palm of his right hand. For less than a second he inadvertently looks into the sun directly overhead and is momentarily blinded. He lets go of the rod and covers both his eyes with his palms.

He stands up and stretches his back, bringing his shoulders up to his ears. He repeats it four or five times. Beads of sweat run down his bald head. He wants to spend some time in the water. He puts one leg over the hull when he sees what looks like a ship in the distance. He closes his eyes and opens them again. The ship is still there.

What are you waiting for? Why don't you come into the water? Baath asks.

I can see a ship out there, Bruno tells Baath. Baath quickly swims to the rudder and pulls himself into the dinghy. Bruno points to the port side. Baath can see it too. It is a ship and it is coming towards the dinghy from the port side. It would cross the dinghy and go to the starboard.

Arre tum sab uppar ao, orders Baath. *Jahaz aa raha hai*. There's a ship coming, get on board quick.

One by one Himanshu, Rama Rao Jr and Rama Rao Sr come into the ship quickly followed by Camille. Baath helps her into the boat.

Take one of the tyres from the side of the boat, instructs Baath. There are three small scooter tyres on either side of the dinghy, to prevent the dinghy from hitting the jetty while it is berthed. They are old tyres worn out with use and discarded.

Cut it into half, he tells Rama Rao Sr who has pulled one of the tyres into the boat and cuts the rope that holds it in place. Himanshu holds the tyre against the floorboard while Rama Rao Sr begins to cut the tyre.

In the distance the ship is coursing steadily towards the dinghy. It is now about three miles away.

Bruno, start flashing the ship, says Baath as he takes off his tee shirt. Arre give me the knife will you, he tells Rama Rao Sr who is struggling with the tyre.

Sir I am cutting the tyre sir. It is difficult. *Gora ke pass ek churi hai, usse le aao*.

Bruno may I borrow your knife, Baath asks Bruno who reaches into his bag and pulls out the knife and gives it to Baath.

Baath holds the tee shirt he has been wearing with one hand and begins to cut away a strip from the bottom part evenly. Bruno begins flashing his camera at the ship.

Rama Rao Sr has cut halfway through the tyre. He is sweating profusely now. Himanshu who is holding the tyre tries to keep his eyes focused on the task Rama Rao Sr is doing. He wants to look at the ship but is afraid if his attention wavers Rama Rao might accidently cut his hand instead of the tyre. The tyre has thin metal bands running through it which is making it difficult to cut through.

Baath picks up the long rod Bruno has been sharpening and asks Rama Rao Jr to give him the can of lube oil. Then he asks Camille if her lighter is working. Camille reaches into her purse and pulls it out and flicks it a couple of times. It is not working.

I have a lighter in my bag, Bruno says. He takes it out and gives it to Baath. Baath flicks it. The lighter works.

Jaldi karo, jaldi karo, he tells Rama Rao Sr. Make it quick! Baath pours lube oil over the strip of the tee shirt he has cut. Some of the oil falls on his hand, and drips on to the floor of the dinghy. Rama Rao has cut through the tyre now. He gives it to Baath who pours some lube oil on it as well. Then he spears the tyre on the rod and ties the tee shirt strip to it and lights it.

The cloth burns bright orange and thick black smoke comes out of the burning tyre. Baath waves the rod and asks Himanshu to hold on to the rod too. Both of them sway the rod backwards and forwards signalling to the ship.

They can see the ship clearly now. It is less than three miles away. It is a cargo ship.

Rama Rao Sr begins to shout at the top of his voice. Rama Rao Jr joins him. Camille is waving with both her hands. Then she picks up a towel and begins waving it back and forth over her head. Bruno is flashing his camera. Rama Rao Sr begins jumping up and down. The dinghy begins to bob with so many people standing and moving around. Thick smoke billows out of the tyre now. The wind blows some of the smoke into Camille's face making her tear up and cough.

The ship is much nearer now. They can see its hull. It is a dark green. Near the waterline it is all red. A part of the propeller is above the water. It is probably an empty cargo ship. They can see no signs that the ship has seen them. The ship keeps steaming on its course.

With this much smoke they can surely see us, Baath tells Bruno. I wonder why they are not changing course.

The ship takes forty five minutes to cross them and sail into the horizon. It does not change course. Baath feels the frustration swell inside him. Everybody looks defeated. For a long time they stare silently at the spot where the ship has disappeared altogether.

Wellington Island

Baath understands Rama Rao's fear of sharks. If you spent hour after hour in the water with nothing to do your mind starts wandering. Twenty years ago at Wellington Island in Cochin where he had gone for the navy's diving officers' course, he had felt the helplessness in being in the water not knowing what was swimming near him. Panic was the companion. Now as he holds the rope by the side of the dinghy he thinks back on those days.

Forty four officers reported at Cochin for the naval diving officers' course. The training lasted eight weeks. By five thirty in the morning the officers had to reach the Ernakulam bridge that spanned the Cochin channel, inflate Gemini rafts, tie it to the pillar that held the bridge, fit the outboard motor, ready it for use and report for physical training which began at six. They wore cotton blues and PT shoes. After exercises their circuit training began. They had to run for a couple of kilometres, stop, do a different set of exercises, run again for a couple of kilometres, stop, do more exercises and then run again. This went on for ten kilometres. It finished at the Ernakulam bridge. When they reached the bridge they proceeded to the spot above which they had tied their Gemini boat, a V-shaped boat with an outboard motor, and jumped into the channel. The pillars of the bridge were thick and five metres tall. They had to jump so they could reach out, grasp the rope that tied the Gemini to the bridge pillar, reach for their diving fins inside the Gemini, put them on, swim around the pillar, come back and then swim to the dive spot.

The dive spot was usually a mile away. The distance from the pillar to the Gemini was at least six to seven metres apart. Against the current. If the tide was ebbing the current was usually around four or five knots. With a current at that speed they had to swim constantly and fin furiously just to stay in one spot and not be carried away by the current. To make headway they had to put in even more effort or be carried away to the sea. If they stopped finning they would immediately be carried away. They had to fin really hard to get round the pillar. Once there they would surge swiftly in the current to the dive spot. They would reach it in ten minutes once they went around the pillar. On other days there would be buoys at the other side of the channel and the instructor would tell them to go around the buoy. If the buoy was forty degrees to the right at ebb tide and the current they would have to take a course ninety degrees so they managed to go around the buoy. Only if they swam this way they would get near enough to the buoy to go around it and come back.

During monsoons the channel would be full of weed and this made swimming difficult. Once a diver went under the hyacinth so he could swim easier underwater. He misjudged the speed of the current and did not know how fast he was going under the water. He surfaced when he had already reached beneath the pontoon. His head hit the pontoon and he lost consciousness and drowned. Divers had to be careful when they swam the channel.

Once they finished the swim and came back there was the mud walk. At the end of the channel there was slush. Their feet sank in the slush up to their thighs, and sometimes even up to their chests. They often felt they would sink in helplessly, the slush rising up to their noses. If the water was high they were lucky; the slush wouldn't be so deep. But if the water was low, the slush would be thick and deep. It was difficult to move in the slush. For the mud walk they wore rubberised boots with lead soles. Each sole weighed one kilogramme. They would fit the lead soles into their boots and put them on. When the instructor was in a bad mood he made them wear more than one sole for each foot. Sometimes they walked with three kg lead on each foot in the deep slush. It all depended on the mood of the instructor. If he barked 'two' it meant two kg per foot. If he barked 'three' it meant six kg of extra weight on their feet. Wearing those heavy boots they had to jump from the bridge into the mud. From a height of five metres into the mud they would sink straight into it. If they jumped with their feet together not only did they sink deeper into the slush but they ran the risk of getting stuck there. They had to jump with their feet as wide apart as possible but not too wide or they would sink to their neck and break a few bones with the impact. When they hit the mud they had to walk about sixty metres in the mud, a little more than twenty five metres each way.

Only if they landed with their feet apart would they be able to prise out one leg and place it in front of the other and move forward, one step at a time. It was a laborious process when the mud came up to their thighs. If they landed with their feet together they stayed that way. Stuck.

The boots came up to their knees. Each boot was tied together with thin ropes that wound up like laces all the way to the top of the boot. If it was not tied this way, securely, they would not be able to extricate it from the mud when the legs sank into it. The boot would be stuck in the mud and the leg would come away separately. It took between an hour to an hour and a half to finish the mud walk.

After that they ate breakfast. There was a tank by the channel. They came up to the tank, washed up and had a modest breakfast. Four slices of bread or whatever it was they picked up from the Navy Mess before they went for the exercises at six in the morning. Afterwards they went for diving. It was not advisable to dive on a full stomach so they ate as little as possible.

With the sun straight above the head if they dived into the Cochin channel, at the depth of twenty five metres it would be pitch dark. On the surface of the water the sun would be shining nice and bright but once they went down they sank into blackness. That was how polluted the channel was. It was a straight descent into hell. As they went down they could see dull spars of light stabbing the darkness. But very quickly they would see nothing, not even objects six inches in front of their faces. Once underwater they had various tasks to do. Open up shackles, fix some nuts and bolts. In utter darkness. They dived in pairs with two lifelines. One was attached to the dive partner and the other to the top. After their first dive the British navy personnel, part of the dive course, said it was like night diving.

Night diving was even worse. Twice a week they did night diving in the same places. Without lights. It was a nightmare. They dived from the mooring buoys without lights. There was always a current flowing there. They could feel it pull at them as they went down. They went down holding a rope. They had to hold the rope all the time. If they let go they would get carried away by the current underwater. They would drift away into the darkness. It would be impossible to swim back to the same place in the darkness. To stay an hour down there without lights took a lot of courage. They never knew what was around them in the dark waters. Very few survived the experience.

In the first two weeks of the course the ones who would not make it dropped out or were weeded out. At the end of the two weeks only four were left from the forty four who had come for the course.

Baath did not complete his course because he broke his knee in an accident. He was riding pillion and the motorcycle crashed head on into a car driven by three youngsters who had been drunk. The parents came to the hospital to visit Baath and his friend the next day. Baath didn't register a case. But he was out of the diving course.

Seabird

Rama Rao Jr hears the bird as it alights on the dinghy. There is a flutter of wings and there it is, suddenly perched on the framework where the tarpaulin should have been. It is black, silhouetted against the night sky. Rama Rao is sitting right below it. The bird shakes its wings and holds them open for a few moments. It looks as though it is in prayer. The smaller feathers turn in the breeze. Then the bird pecks at its chest, fluffs it out and slowly closes its wings. The bird itself is small, slightly bigger than a pigeon. The bird pays no attention to Rama Rao Jr, its eyes fixed on the horizon. Then it seems to Rama Rao that the bird is withdrawing into itself.

In a flash Rama Rao Jr reaches out and catches the bird. His hands have grasped one of its legs. The bird offers no resistance. Then it frantically begins flapping its wings. In the silence of the night the sound of the wings beating against the bamboo support of the tarpaulin sounds unnaturally loud. Camille who is sleeping on the plank wakes up with a start. Rama Rao Jr has managed to hold the bird with both his hands now. He has caught hold of one of the wings. The other wing keeps flapping. Baath and the others have woken up too. Rama Rao Jr manoeuvres and manages to catch hold of the other wing as well. Now the bird is fully in his grasp. The bird blinks in his hand, as it looks around wildly. The bird feels warm in his hand.

Let's roast this bird, says Rama Rao Jr, looking happy.

Rama Rao Sr moves towards him, and looks greedily at the bird. He is smiling as well.

Let's roast this bird, Rama Rao Jr repeats. We have lube oil we have the tanker top. We can make a fire and roast this bird and we can all eat it. All we have to do is remove its feathers. Some of the feathers of the bird have already fallen out in the struggle.

Camille looks at Baath and says, Baath there is no way we are going to kill this poor bird.

You can't kill this bird, Baath tells Rama Rao Jr.

Kyon nahin mar sakte hai? Rama Rao Jr asks. He sounds defiant. Why can't I kill this bird?

Yes, I am hungry too. This bird is making me even more hungry. We should kill this bird immediately and eat it, says Rama Rao Sr.

How much meat are you going to get if you kill this little bird? Baath asks Rama Rao Jr. Two hundred grammes of meat? Look at it. It is a thin and small bird, smaller than a large pigeon.

Rama Rao Jr lifts the bird and examines it. He has caught the bird so tight in his hands that it cannot even struggle.

Baath continues, When you divide it how much is each of us going to eat. Remember that we are now used to not eating food. Our stomachs are not expecting any food. But once you eat this bird, your stomach will demand more food. You will feel hungry. Very hungry. What will you do then? Will more birds come and sit for you to catch and kill?

You are telling him not to kill the bird only because madam *ne bola hai*, because madam told you so, Sr Rama Rao interjects angrily.

All madam has said is that this bird is a sign of good luck. If we kill this bird only bad luck will follow. So far we have been lucky. We have been lucky not to capsize, we have been lucky to have been alive. Our water is running out. We could do with a little good luck right now. We cannot kill this bird.

Rama Rao is furious now. He points to Bruno Beauregard and says, Ever since this man has come on board the only luck we've had is bad luck sahib. This bird is not bad luck, this man is bad luck. We can kill the bird.

Yes sir, this bird has willingly come to us. It is a sign we should eat it, says Rama Rao Jr. We should kill it. I'm so hungry I could eat it raw.

Look here Ramiah, how many days have we survived without food?

Four nights and five days sir.

Did you expect to survive this long?

No sir.

Haven't we also weathered a storm, a big one, a really bad one?

Yes sir, says Rama Rao.

You know how bad it was. Did you think we could last this long without food? But we have. The storm was so bad that we wouldn't have lasted through it even if we had food. This bird is a messenger of good luck. Killing it will end our run of good luck. We can't kill this messenger. We must pay heed to the message. It is a message that our luck is turning for the better. Please let the bird go.

Sr Rama Rao is silent now. He does not look at Rama Rao Jr.

Please let the bird go, says Baath. Rama Rao Jr looks helplessly at the bird and reluctantly relaxes his grip. In a hurried flutter of wings the bird flies into the dark night. Rama Rao Jr sits silently. He is not entirely convinced of Baath's argument but there is nothing he can do except to try and ignore the hunger gnawing viciously at him now.

Himanshu lies down and cradles the back of his head on his palms. He looks up at the sky. It is full of stars. He can see a shooting star. Then he sees a light that moves much slower across the sky. He draws Baath's attention to it and asks: Is that a plane?

Baath, happy for the diversion, looks at it for a couple of seconds and says, Yes, that's a plane. It's probably going from South East Asia to Sri Lanka or further west. Port Blair is a reporting point for the planes.

Baath then looks at Bruno who is also watching the plane go across the sky. The plane is now almost directly overhead but very high.

Bruno, why don't you switch on your underwater camera and flash it in the sky, suggests Baath.

Baath, that damn thing is probably flying at thirty five thousand feet. From that height do you think they will see the flash? Bruno asks rhetorically. Then he answers his own question. Of course they will not see the flash.

Doesn't matter. But what if they do? Should we not try everything we can?

Bruno laughs cynically. But he pulls out the camera and the flash and switches the flash on and waits for it to get into the standby mode. He flashes once, then twice and then a couple of times more. In the sky the aircraft is moving on. Soon the only thing they can see in the sky are stars. Thousands of them. More stars than they have ever seen in their lives.

Okha

Baath thinks of the seabird he coaxed Rama Rao Jr to let go. He is hungry enough now to eat it alive. Life had turned an ironic full circle. Before his diving course, Baath had been posted in Okha, Gujarat. Initially during his posting, he was sent out to Porbandar where the Navy maintained a small detachment.

Baath was the officer in charge. He divided his time between Porbandar and Okha. One of his duties was to go on to an American oil rig that was drilling ninety nautical miles off Okha in the Arabian Sea. The rig was on lease to the Oil and Natural Gas Corporation. Navy kept tabs on the rig because it was on waters where the sea boundary with Pakistan was unsettled. Islamabad kept complaining that the rig was on its waters and regularly sent helicopters and ships to intimidate those on the rig. They often tried to land helicopters onto the helipad on the rig.

Baath went on to the rig on a Russian helicopter, owned by the British Airways, a Sikorsky 76. Whenever the helicopter took off from the rig, those on the rig would hurriedly arrange oil drums on the helipad in such a way that Pakistani helicopters wouldn't have space to land there. When Baath's helicopter went to the rig, it radioed ahead that it was coming. The drums would be removed while his helicopter hovered in the air above.

The Pakistanis would often send their ships to circle the rig. They wanted to force the rig off those waters. They harassed and intimidated those on the rig so they would leave demoralized. The navy posted two soldiers from the naval analysis unit, the intelligence branch, on the rig. Their job was to note the time and date and the nature of the aggressive overtures and prepare reports on these incidents. These reports went to the western navy command in Bombay. The Pakistanis kept the naval intelligence on the rig so active that Baath had been given the duty of going to the rig twice a week and collecting the reports. The helicopter was the lifeline to the rig. It was also used for rotation and change of personnel.

The man in charge of the rig was a friendly American. He was responsible for stocking the rig with provisions and food. He told Baath to let him know if he wanted anything from the rig. Baath went a number of times, sometimes taking gifts with him for the American. He chatted with the British pilots who stayed in Lalbagh Palace, a guest house. There were four British personnel there, two pilots and two for technical support. Two of the Britons brought their families along with them to stay in the guest house. All their Scotch and salami came from the rig. They bought it off the Americans. Later for some reason the Brits fell out with the Americans and requested Baath to get the provisions for them from the rig. Baath asked the American in charge if he could buy some provisions off him. He didn't mind selling Baath whatever he wanted. Baath paid the American with the dollars the Brits gave him. Everything he bought was packed and loaded into the helicopter. The Brits took what they wanted and Baath took what he wanted. It worked out fine for everybody. Occasionally Baath would give the American a bird he had shot at Porbandar.

Porbandar had many salt pans which attracted migratory birds of all kinds, ducks, curlews, ibis, teals, flamingos. There were so many of them that Naval aircraft positioned at the airport there found it difficult to take off every day for sorties. The ground staff had guns to scare the birds away so they didn't get in the way whenever the aircraft took off or landed. The planes flew many sorties and were often in the air. The airport manager had a twelve bore gun and a lot of ammunition to shoot the birds.

Baath and his men had their own guns, the SLRs and the higher calibre guns. These were no good for shooting birds if they wanted to eat them afterwards. With that calibre of ammunition, there would be nothing left of the birds once they were hit but a messy mangle of blood and feathers. The airport manager was not using his twelve bore. He suggested Baath could use it to shoot the birds with it if he wanted. It would get rid of some of the troublesome birds and Baath would get his birds in one piece. The twelve bore rifle shot cartridges with pellets in them. Each cartridge had different markings with numbers like 'six', 'four' or 'eight'. If there was a flock of birds to shoot at, the thing to do would be to use number six. A twelve bore with number six sprayed many pellets at flying birds. The process was simple. The pellet hit the bird and the bird fell down. Sometimes they shot a number six cartridge at a covey of ducks and four would fall. The lesser the number on the cartridge the lesser the pellets in it. The higher the number the more the pellets. The trick was to point the twelve bore at the middle of the flock or towards the leading bird in the flock and fire. The pellets spread out a bit on their way up. Some found their birds and the birds would fall. They went out to where they had fallen to collect them. It was more difficult to track wounded birds that frantically fluttered on only to fall dead later.

Once Baath went for a duck shoot with the Brits and shot a pelican instead. The bird was so big that it had to be slung over the shoulder to be taken to the truck. The man who carried the pelican held it by its legs over his shoulder. All the way to the truck, the giant beak of the bird scraped the ground. They weighed the meat they got out of the bird after it was cut and cleaned. Six kilos. It was tough meat even after it was cooked. Tougher than duck. But they enjoyed it.

Hundreds of pigeons lived in the building where Baath's office was located. It was a large cavernous room. The pigeons sat everywhere on the ledges and on the window sills. All day they flew about billing and cooing. Their droppings lay everywhere. Pigeon feathers flew about when they switched on the dusty fan. Baath sometimes wondered what would happen if a pigeon hit the fan as it spun but they managed to somehow steer clear of it. In the beginning it was difficult to adjust to so many pigeons for company but soon Baath got used to it. He didn't mind the noise they made. He gave his personal attendant standing instructions on the pigeons. The instruction was to catch four or five of the pigeons. Everyday. It wasn't very difficult. All the attendant had to do after it became dark was to prop a ladder up against the wall leading up to the places the pigeons roosted. He climbed the ladder with a torch and reached out and caught the pigeon he wanted and brought it down and snapped its neck. Then he went up the ladder for the next one. Every day he caught and killed four pigeons one after the other in this fashion. Then plucked their feathers, cut them, cleaned them and roasted them over a fire. It was great to snack on with the alcohol Baath got from the defence canteen or from the rig.

Two things were difficult to get in Porbandar, the town where Mahatma Gandhi was born. Meat and alcohol. For four pegs of alcohol you could get a lot done in Porbandar. There was a retired army colonel who was in charge of a chemical factory. He was entitled to defence liquor but there was no defence canteen in Porbandar. The nearest defence canteen was in faraway Jamnagar. When he learnt that Baath had come to set up a naval detachment there, the colonel immediately came to Baath's office in a jeep and hugged him fiercely as the pigeons flapped around them. He told Baath if he took mercy on him and gave him four bottles of whiskey every month he would open his company guest house to Baath or his family or his friends, even his friends' friends. Any time of the day or night. They could stay as long as they wished.

Ration broiler and mutton were not available all the time. Okha was quite a godforsaken place that way, more a village than a town. If Baath wanted to eat ice cream they had to travel ten kilometres to Meeta Khadi, three kilometres from Dwaraka. There was no shortage of seafood though. Baath employed two boys from a fishing village as his detachment help. Their fathers were fishermen. Through the boys Baath got whatever he wanted, fish or prawns or crabs. He ate any fish he wanted. He shot any bird he wanted. He ate everything he wanted. Now in the middle of the Andaman Sea he drank water twice a day to stay alive.

Rutland Island

In December 2000, Prabhakar, the son of a governor of a north eastern state came to Port Blair from Bombay and got in touch with Baath. He wanted to go diving off Rutland Island. And he didn't want to go by dinghy. He had brought his nephew, Nikhil, along. Nikhil was a well-built young man who wore a body hugging tee shirt, shorts and oversized sunglasses. Baath hired a big boat for the dive. They set out from Chidiyatapoo at nine in the morning. Clouds hung low in the sky above them and small waves lapped against the steep stone steps leading into the sea. The water was murky with sand that churned up and clumps of floating seaweed. The big boat was anchored a little distance away so it wouldn't get grounded in the shallow waters. They got to the bigger boat on a dinghy which they reached by wading into the sea. After they clambered aboard the big boat, it set off with the dinghy in tow. Two minutes into the journey the youngster took off his tee shirt and was down to his shorts. He flexed his muscles and slowly and carefully rubbed sun tan cream all over himself even though there was no sun overhead. He was oblivious to everything else around him. His uncle took out a camera and began to take pictures of the receding shore and of his nephew thoughtfully applying the sun tan. The big boat was bobbing up and down in the waves.

Once they crossed Munda Pahad, ten minutes later, the sea widened and the waves came on bigger. They started to bear the brunt of the monsoon. The boat began to pitch up and down in the waves. As the boat eased out to the channel out of Chidiyatapoo, the tone of the engine changed, the sea shifted and all at once the boat began to roll in the waves as well. The waves now reared up more than a metre and a half and a little later they rose two metres out of the sea. The boat began pitching and rolling in a kind of corkscrew motion. Soon the nephew was lying flat on the bench. The motion of the boat had made him seasick. Then he got up covering his mouth with the palm of his hand steadying himself with the other hand and stumbled to the side of the boat, held the railing, leaned out and began to retch and vomit. He became silent and his uncle moved next to him and began rubbing his back and gave him water to drink.

Baath asked if they still wanted to continue for the dive in this weather. Nikhil began to shake his head but his uncle raised his hand and said they should continue. Baath suggested that they could dive at Wandoor which was somewhat protected from the rough sea. They wouldn't see big fish there but they would see a lot of small fish and there was an extensive coral fringe there. The nephew shook his head without saying a word but his uncle said they should carry on and that he wanted to dive only in Rutland at Surmai Mundi. He had come all the way from Bombay to do just that and he couldn't turn back now considering Surmai Mandi was only an hour away. He wanted to see the big fish. His nephew did not want to see anything now. He just wanted to lie down on the bench and look at the grey sky thickening with clouds.

Surmai Mundi was off the north east part of Rutland Island,

a little over eight nautical miles from Chidiyatapoo, in the open sea. Big fish swam in Surmai Mundi. A diver could see them all around, sharks, groupers, Napoleon fish. Cinq Island lay three and a half nautical miles further south, across the Manners Strait, a channel. When they reached Surmai Mundi, Baath and Prabhakar got into the dinghy and set off to the dive spot, after telling the crew the axis along which they would dive and where they would surface. He instructed that the boat reach the area and told the crew to keep a lookout for them when they surfaced. Ketu, the dinghy master came in the dinghy along with Himanshu and another man. When they descended into the sea for the dive, the visibility was between six to seven metres. The current was strong and the sea was flowing in the same direction as well. This meant that they would finish the dive far sooner than they had anticipated.

It was a decent dive and they saw some barracudas and a big school of trevallies and some groupers and a giant turtle swimming swiftly southwards in the current. They didn't have to put in effort to fin. It was as though they were being pulled by an invisible hand through the water. After thirty five minutes Baath indicated to Prabhakar that it was time they surfaced. He was worried if they drifted in the current any further they would get carried to the centre of the channel. Prabhakar shook his head and began showing Baath his pressure gauge indicating that he had lot of air left and therefore they should continue. Baath tried to tell Prabhakar that the currents at the centre of Manners Strait were very strong and if they went any further they wouldn't be able to rendezvous with the boat which had been given specific directions where to go and wait and keep a look out for the divers when they surfaced. Prabhakar was not willing to give up the dive. Even as they debated they drifted further underwater away from where the boat was to pick them up. Prabhakar kept pointing to the pressure gauge. Baath had more air left in his tank and he showed Prabhakar the pressure gauge reading. They argued some more. Finally Baath got fed up and began to surface and Prabhakar had no choice but to follow. They surfaced more than a hundred metres from the shore behind the boat and they began drifting towards the centre of the channel. They could see the boat but the people in the boat couldn't see them. Baath inflated the bright yellow safety balloon and they began to shout to the boat. The wind snatched at their voices and the sea crashed around and over them. The waves were so big that for the most part they couldn't see the boat and couldn't hear anything over the sea which was relentlessly pulling them farther and farther away from the boat. They couldn't see the dinghy but Baath assumed that it would be on the other side of the boat, near the shoreline where they ought to have surfaced.

Baath indicated to Prabhakar that they should head for the shore. They struck out diagonally backwards in the hope they would curve with the current and be able to tread water near the shore. It was a slow and exhausting swim and when they neared the shore, it was actually the rock line. The sand line was further away. The waves were crashing against the rocks and after they crossed the outer line of breakers they could feel the waves surge towards them and carry them swiftly towards the rocks. Fighting the oncoming waves, they scrambled on to the rocks, removed their buoyancy jackets and oxygen tanks and placed the equipment on top of the rocks, above the reach of the big waves. It was around eleven in the morning.

They clambered over the sharp rocks slippery with moss and algae and headed for the shore line which was still some distance away, carrying the equipment as they negotiated their way carefully. The sand was coarse and full of broken shells which cut into their feet. Crabs scurried away all around them. Once they reached the shoreline they headed for the tree line and placed their equipment there. They couldn't see the dinghy in the sea so they headed along the shore northwards round the bay. Here Rutland rose steep over them as they made their way through the rocky coastline. Rutland was tallest on the eastern parts, where Mt Ford angled 435 metres over the hundred kilometre island, overlooking the mangroves, the bays, the rocky inlets and the forests where the tribals, the Jangil of Rutland, had become a minor footnote in history towards 1920.

Once they went round the bend of the bay they could see the dinghy still near the rock where they were supposed to surface. They could see the safety balloon bobbing up and down with the wave crests. The dinghy was not too far away and Himanshu and Ketu were looking the other way. Baath and Prabhakar started waving and shouting. After a while Himanshu turned and noticed them on the shore. He swam ashore with life jackets and fins and made his way over the slippery rocks. It took a while for him to reach the shore and when he reached they discussed the situation. They knew getting to the beach was easier than getting to the boat. The waves were coming on big. The dinghy was anchored beyond the breakers. If it came any nearer it would get carried by the waves and get smashed against the rocks. Yet, they had to make an attempt to reach the dinghy. There was no other way. Himanshu gave his life jacket and a mask to Prabhakar and they decided to make a go of it. It was tricky. They had to go over the rocks where the waves were rushing in, crawling part of the way as the rocks cut them. When they finally got past the breakers they struck out towards the dinghy and clambered aboard. There was now no question of a second dive.

Ketu and his assistant started pulling the anchor up as soon as they were all in the dinghy. It was a thin wire anchor and though they tried to pull it up it wouldn't come up. Ketu realized that the anchor had wedged itself in the rocks below and no matter what he tried he couldn't dislodge it. The sea was surging against the dinghy and pushing it as well. Baath told Ketu that he would dive down and free the anchor and once it was free Ketu should immediately start the engine while his assistant pulled up the anchor and head out to sea while Baath surfaced and climbed onto the dinghy. They were less than seventy metres from the sharp rocks. Baath then dived into the sea to find the anchor and free it. It was only four metres deep and it was all smooth rock sloping upwards towards the beach. He found the anchor wedged against the rocks and struggled to free it and once it was done he shot up. His lungs were aching as he surfaced and saw the dinghy drifting rapidly towards the rocks. Baath couldn't hear the engine. He held on to the side of the dinghy as it passed and started shouting to Ketu to start the dinghy quickly. Ketu could not start the dinghy. There was something wrong with the crank handle. The lock wasn't working. He fitted the handle and yanked it up hard again. The engine kicked back, roared and sputtered out, and the handle flew over Baath's head and fell into the sea and sank. The dinghy was now much nearer the rocks.

Baath shouted to Ketu and Himanshu instructing them to throw the big anchor as well as the medium-sized anchor overboard so the dinghy could get some purchase on the smooth rock gradient below. Ketu threw the bigger anchor with three large curving hooks into the sea. Himanshu threw the medium sized anchor. Neither anchor caught the rocks. They slid over the slippery rock, trailing as the dinghy rapidly approached the cluster of rocks that jutted viciously out of the sea.

Baath told the others to quickly wear life jackets, put on their fins and masks and jump into the sea before the dinghy smashed against the rocks. He let go of the dinghy and began to swim away from it and saw Himanshu, Ketu and Prabhakar jump into the sea just as the dinghy, riding a huge swelling wave, smashed into the rocks. The stern portion of the dinghy hit the rocks with a mighty sound and split open. When the wave receded the dinghy went back into the sea, taking in water in the stern. It now began to tilt as the next wave threw it back against the rocks. With every wave it smashed against the crags and somehow one of the anchors managed to cling on to the bedrock underneath but it was too late. Baath and Himanshu took Prabhakar to the shore and swam back to the dinghy to help salvage what they could. They made four trips to the boat. By now things which could float were floating all around them. The dinghy was sinking deeper into the sea. They salvaged the tanks, the regulators, and the BCDs. They lost some masks, fins and weight belts. Now the stern portion of the dinghy that housed the engine sank into the sea and only the prow was sticking out above the waves. The dinghy was thirty feet long and only four feet of it slanted out of the sea at an angle, the waves foaming around the portion above the water.

The wind was whipping the sea at around fifteen knots an hour now and the clouds had massed thick but it was not raining. All around them the sky was deepening into dark grey. Baath sent Ketu out along the beach to where the bigger boat was anchored out in the bay where the sea was a little calmer. He walked more than two kilometres around the bend and signaled the boat to come around to the part where the others were. The boat came around opposite the beach where they waited. It anchored 200 metres away. If it came any nearer it would get smashed against the rocks like the dinghy. Left to themselves, Ketu, Baath and Himanshu still had the energy to strike out to the boat but Prabhakar was all of a sudden exhausted. All they had was a couple of bottles of water which they found in the dinghy before it sank. It was two thirty in the afternoon now and they were hungry and wondering how to get to the boat when they saw a huge dinghy out in the sea going fishing.

The big dinghy was towing a smaller one. The smaller dinghy was piled high with fishing nets. The boat signalled to the dinghy and got it to come alongside and explained the predicament to the fishermen requesting them to pick up those in the shore. The smaller dinghy could approach the rocks but it did not have an engine. It had to be rowed.

From the shore as they watched, they could see four or five well-built fishermen get into the dinghy. They began rowing towards the first line of breakers. When they were seventy metres away from the shore, they dropped anchor. One of them stood up and began gesturing to those on the shore to swim up to the breakers. Ketu and his assistant were also given life jackets and they left their equipment near the tree line and began to traverse the sand once again towards the sharp rocks and crashing waves. The waves were foaming all over the rocks and they began to crawl on the rocks, slippery with moss and sharp with barnacles growing on them. Because they were wearing masks they could see a little in the front as they inched forward, bleeding from the many cuts the rocks and the barnacles inflicted on their knees, palms, shins and thighs.

The salt water from the sea made their cuts worse. Ketu and his assistant had been wearing lungis which they had discarded because they were cumbersome and were now down to their underpants. Because they were wearing fins, the progress was slow. They needed the fins to swim against the powerful waves that kept pushing them back on to the rocks. Like seals they crawled, desperate to reach the dinghy, across the last rocks and plunged into the furious sea.

When they reached the fishermen pulled them into the dinghy one by one. Prabhakar was the first to clamber aboard. He rested against the fishing nets, gasping for breath, his chest heaving. By the time they reached the big boat and got onto it, the blood had started oozing in tiny rivulets from the bigger cuts. The rescuers refused to take anything for their troubles and set off again to the spot they were going to fish. The big boat weighed anchor and headed for Chidiyatapoo. The sun had begun to sink into the sea from behind the clouds.

At Chidiyatapoo the gradient is very gradual and by the time they reached, around six thirty, night had enveloped everything. As the boat anchored at a safe distance they could see the lights at the shop on the shore twinkling in the dark. But there was no way to get to the pier because there was no dinghy with them now. They were all very hungry. All they had eaten was some biscuits that were there in the boat. The nephew was not seasick any longer. There were two torches on the big boat which they used to signal towards the shop. After about half an hour of signalling the owner of the shop, Bala understood there was some problem and came out to the big boat on a dinghy. '*Kya ho gaya sahib? Dinghy kahan gaya?*' What happened? Where is the dinghy?

Baath responded: *Arrey! Pehle yeh batao, dookan mein dettol vettol hai kya*? First of all tell me, do you have Dettol in your shop?

When Baath reached his house in Sahajeevan colony late that night the first thing he did was take a hot bath and empty an entire bottle of dettol to salve the cuts on his body. He counted more than a hundred.

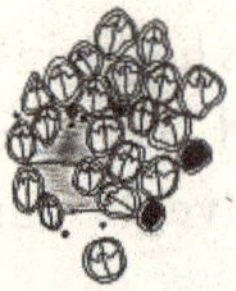

Barnacles

I'm so hungry that I could have eaten that bird alive, Baath confides to Camille.

What happened to your chewing gum?

Rama Rao is sharing it with Himanshu.

I am sorry I don't have any left.

It's okay.

Camille is looking at the fish darting around her in the transparent blue waters.

Well these fish are eating off your dinghy.

Really? Anything edible down there?

There are lots of barnacles growing on your dinghy. As Captain Haddock keeps saying: billions of blue blistering barnacles!

Captain Haddock?

You know, from Tintin.

Camille pronounces it the French way, taintain, nasally.

Taintain? Baath asks. He is slightly perplexed.

The comic book with the young reporter and the bearded Captain Haddock and the dog Snowy. How could you not know. You could be mistaken for Captain Haddock yourself. They are written by Herge.

Right. I think Karan, my elder son, reads them.

You've got billions of barnacles down here Captain Haddock. How long has it been since you had the dinghy bottom cleaned?

It hasn't been cleaned for some time.

Baath, how hungry are you?

I could eat anything right now.

What is the most adventurous thing that you have eaten, asks Camille.

That's a tough one. After a while Baath says, I've eaten pelican once.

No you haven't, Camille shrieks in surprise and shock.

Yes I have.

It sounds illegal to me. Was it any good?

It was excellent.

Do restaurants serve pelican meat here?

I don't see any restaurants here, Baath says looking around.

Not here Baath. You know what I mean. In India?

No. I shot one while I was posted in Okha. Please don't say the word restaurant. It is making me hungry.

Okha?

Yes. Okha.

You shot pelican in Russia?

No. In Gujarat. Okha is in Gujarat. Gujarat is a state in the north west coast of India. I've also eaten snake. Although I can't say I enjoyed that as much as the pelican.

Was it snake made the Chinese way?

No. I ate it practically uncooked.

Really?

Well, half cooked. We had to eat snakes for our survival course while I was training to be a navy commando. We had to catch these things and roast it over a fire and eat them.

It sounds disgusting.

Well, you eat frog's legs as a delicacy, don't you? That used to sound disgusting to me. But now I am ready to try even that. In fact I think if that bird landed again I would personally catch it and eat it along with its feathers.

If you are that hungry why don't you try eating some of these barnacles that are growing on your dinghy. Camille runs her hands underwater over the hull of the dinghy. There are hundreds of barnacles growing on the hull of the dinghy. The tiny fish are looking for food among the barnacles.

Baath swims along the dinghy underwater. All along the bottom of the dinghy hundreds of barnacles have formed. They are in clusters. He reaches out and touches them. They are like clam shells. He swims back to Camille.

There's lots of them down here. Are they edible?

We ordered barnacles in a restaurant in Spain once.

You said restaurant again.

Sorry.

Never mind. Did you eat it?

No. Why would I? But my companion did.

Baath calls across to Bruno who is sharpening the rod.

Bruno there are barnacles down here growing on the boat? Are these edible?

I've never eaten barnacles, says Bruno.

Restaurants in Spain serve them.

Yeah? Bruno asks skeptically. Maybe Camille has a good recipe for these.

Camille does not answer Bruno directly.

I remember asking the restaurant how they cooked it because I was curious, she tells Baath. They boil the barnacle along with bayleaf. I think they put in a dash of wine and flavor. Paprika it was I think.

Bayleaf? In India too we use a lot of that to cook.

Do you cook Baath?

I can cook a basic fish.

Really? How do you do that? Camille asks challengingly.

You know sometimes when I take people diving my boys catch fish. We trail a lure when we travel and the boys fish while we dive. When you catch the fish you skewer the fish with a long stick. You put four fish in each skewer after cleaning them out with a small cut. Then you set up three or four skewers two to two and a half feet above a fire. While you dive one of the boys will turn the skewers. If you catch groupers, they have thick skin and do not burn easily, but they cook the best. The fish cook slowly over about three hours. All you need then is a knife. You know you can find these plants which we call jungli lassoon, wild garlic plant. If you cut open its stem they open like Styrofoam sheets. You can use them as plates. You cut into the fish. There will be white cooked flesh inside. You eat it just like that. With salad. Some fresh lime, onion and cucumber. It is the best meal in the world.

Wow, says Camille. That sounds tasty. Why didn't you cook it this way for us?

I promise the next time you come to Andamans I will.

It looks as though there is not going to be a next time.

I don't agree. There always is a next time. There always will be a next time. The next time we will go to Havelock Island for a dive. I know the people who run the resort at Radhanagar beach very well.

Isn't that where there was a crocodile attack?

Yes.

Why would you suggest a place that has seen a crocodile attack?

Don't worry. They caught the crocodile and put it in the zoo near where I live in Port Blair. It's not going to do you any harm.

What happened? Why did it attack?

I was there the next day on the Bambooka.

Bambooka?

It's an inter-island passenger ferry that I captain between Port Blair and Havelock. I was in Havelock the day after the attack. The head of police there is a friend of mine. He told me the story.

What is the story?

When we go back to Port Blair, I will tell you. Now is not the time.

Your life here must be interesting.

It's kind of fun, but sometimes it can be trying and you never know when things will turn. Once we went for a dive off Rutland Island with this guy who insisted we go to a particular spot to dive. It went badly. I will tell you that story as well, but not now. It will ruin my appetite.

Camille lapses into silence. Then she looks at Baath and says, Well, if you are going to eat the barnacles now, we'll have to manage without the wine and the bay leaf and the paprika for now. We will save the wine and the bay leaf for your next time.

In this case, the next time will be in a restaurant. Maybe in Spain. How do you eat these things?

Don't ask me. I am not going to eat them. You are the one who is hungry enough to eat them.

Are they safe to eat?

I guess so. You will know when you eat them anyway. I think it is somewhere between a crustacean and a mollusk. It will be like eating raw shrimp. Just think you are eating sushi.

Damn good. Show me how.

Camille scratches the side of the boat with her long nails and removes a barnacle from the hull of the dinghy. She pulls open the shell and shows it to Baath. Inside a tiny creature wriggles and moves.

See that? she says, that's the thing you have to eat.

Really? Can it be eaten?

It is waiting for you to eat it. It's the bounty of the sea. In Europe you will pay a hefty price for this.

Baath looks skeptically at the tiny wriggling animal. It is less than a quarter of a centimetre.

You take it out with your finger and eat it. Go ahead.

Baath takes it out and puts it in his mouth. It is crunchy but it is hardly anything to eat. It tastes as though he has bitten a raw crab shell by mistake. It is insubstantial as well. Camille collects a few more barnacles and takes out the creatures from inside them and gives them to Baath. He puts it in his mouth and chews.

Himanshu is watching him chew the animal inside the barnacles.

Sahib taste kaisa hai?

Theek hai, kha sakte ho.

For about an hour nobody else eats the barnacles. Then Himanshu plucks a barnacle off the hull and puts it in his mouth. The rest of the day they are all pulling barnacles off the dinghy, prising open the shell and eating them, one by one.

The Divers

A travel agent in Port Blair asked Baath if he could take a couple of his clients out diving. The agent said he'd more than compensate him. Baath knew he had to find a job. The payout from his retirement would soon run out. He was diving for fun until then. But he had never taken people out for dives on a commercial basis, although he was a qualified dive instructor from the navy. The agent said he constantly got enquiries for dives. Baath thought that he might as well learn more about commercial diving. He had already got some of the equipment by then and Mona and Baath had begun to dive for fun, taking their friends along. Baath agreed to take the two Britons out diving.

He took them to Cinq Island from Chidiyatapoo. Mona came along, as did John, another British tourist. They left early in the day and did a couple of dives off Cinq; they began their return journey a little early because the sea was getting choppy and the wind sharp. By the time they got to Rutland the sea became calmer. The sun was not about to set yet. So they anchored in one of the bays off Rutland to catch some fish. A fine rain was falling. John produced a bottle of red wine from his bag. They drank the wine in plastic disposable cups and caught some fish in the rain, a barracuda, a grouper. It was not a bad experience. Baath began to think seriously about diving as a commercial venture.

Baath had bought some more equipment from a commercial diving establishment in the Lacadive Islands which had taken a small building on lease at Wandoor, right on the beachfront where they stored their diving equipment and filled the diving tanks. That dive company found it difficult to manage the operation in far flung Andaman and the owner handed it all over to Baath to run it anyway he wanted to. To Baath, this seemed a logical step. He began to take tourists out for dives. He learnt with every dive how to handle tourists underwater. Most of them were first-time divers. He told them what to expect underwater, what they would see and how they should behave, how to signal underwater and how not to drift off on their own and how not to panic underwater.

One day the former owner called to say his dive instructor, Bruno Beauregard, a senior dive instructor, wanted to come down to Andamans for a few days to go diving. Baath told him that Bruno was welcome and he would take him out diving. Baath was told that Bruno would come along with his companion, Camille Pascal from Paris. Baath said that would be no problem. He was not going to charge them. It was agreed that Bruno would pay for whatever running expenses there would be for the dinghy for the duration of their dives.

On the third of March, Bruno and Camille landed in Port Blair and checked into Bay Island Hotel, the best hotel in town. It had a stunning view of the channel that led to the harbor. It sat on a steep incline that fell into the sea. A path snaked down to the waterline, where there was a private jetty for the hotel. Bruno and Camille could hear the dull wash of the sea in their room which overlooked the waters that glinted blue and yellow in the sunlight. On the evening they arrived Mona and Baath met them in the hotel to discuss the diving they would do and decided to start diving from Wandoor, where the dive center was. Bruno and Camille moved into the forest guest house at Chidiyatapoo. The guest house overlooked the waters across Rutland Island. There was a well-maintained lawn on one side. A low aquamarine wrought iron fence ran along the side of the lawn. Beyond it the hill on which the guest house stood dropped off and fell into the sea amidst a profusion of trees and plants. In front of the low single-storied guest house stretched an open verandah which had red plastic chairs beneath and a fine, uninterrupted view of the bay. In the far distance, across the Manners Strait they could see the loom of the islands that lay beyond. The verandah ran all along the front leading off into the rooms along it. The room which they were given had two cots that huddled together in the centre; the room was large and had a false wooden flooring. Cupboards were built into one of the walls and a rudimentary dressing table stood in a corner. On the window that looked out of the room into the backyard hung faded curtains with pink floral pattern. The bathroom didn't have a water heater. The single fan whirled noisily at low speed all night.

They dived around Wandoor; they didn't see big fish but they saw some coral. The following day they went to Rutland Island; Baath shifted all the dive equipment to Chidiyatapoo, to a tea shop across the road from where concrete steps led into the lapping water, clumps of seaweed showing at low tide. Baath knew the owner, Bala, who let him keep the dive equipment in a room at the back of the shop. The waters around Chidiyatapoo teemed with fish, and there were corals too. The following day they went to Cinq. On the first dive they spotted a huge stingray resting under a rock. Baath had seen stingrays before. Often in the area manta rays swam along the surface. Some of them were enormous. Baath was afraid of the stingrays and stayed away from their curving tails that grew into a spear. Bruno showed no fear; he went right up to the sting ray, got down in front of it, and began to pet it under the flap. The sting ray twitched, moved from under the rock and turned toward Bruno. Then it began to glide along the sea bottom. Baath could see its eyes blink periodically. Bruno reached out and continued to pet the stingray turning gently away from it. The stingray rose slowly towards the surface of the sea where the sun was streaming into the water in broad columns, its wing flapping gently. As it floated past Camille, Bruno took pictures of the sting ray and Camille together. It was a blotched sting ray with a thick tail that tapered into a blade with teeth running on either side of it. Its upper surface was a patchy purple, black and brown. The wing span was easily eight feet across. As it passed by, Bruno swam towards it. The sting ray flapped its way upwards. As it swum away Bruno could see its white underside, its mouth curving as though in a smile.

They saw a long green moray eel swim out of a craggy coral. Its mouth was rapidly opening and closing displaying its ragged set of long teeth. But it whirled around abruptly and swam back in as soon as the divers approached. They waited for it to reappear from its burrow. After a while it peeped out, its beady eyes staring at them from its round head and then it disappeared into the crevasse again. Yellowfin fusiliers shot into view. They were a big school, hundreds of them darted this way and that and quickly disappeared into the sea. On the seabed a foot long sea cucumber rooted among the dead corals in slow motion. Parrot fish hung suspended in the water then gently swam along. A big trigger fish came up to the divers for an inspection and hovered around. Baath could see its teeth through its open mouth. A school of slender ladyfish glinted near a large brain coral.

They did a second dive along the northern coast of Cinq Island, on the western side. Here the fish were bigger. They surprised a battery of sawtooth barracudas as soon as they began their dive. A large barracuda about a metre long kept a watch on them without moving. Big black spots splotched its grey sides. Suddenly it dropped through the water to their level and stayed there for a while, showing its nasty teeth that stuck out like sabres. Then it swiveled and was gone in a great burst of speed. A spiky lionfish appeared to rest on a rock at the bottom. As they went closer it drifted away. A couple of big kingfish swam some distance away. Soon other kingfish swam into view, a streaming streak of silver in the sea lit by a bright afternoon sun.

They dove for four days off Cinq and Rutland islands. Everyday early in the morning, Baath rode his Royal Enfield motorcycle twenty-six kilometres from Port Blair to Chidiyatapoo. It took him about three quarters of an hour. There was hardly any traffic at that time of the day. After the dive they would return to Chidiyatapoo. If they returned too late the tide would be out and they would have to wade through the waters among the slush and seaweed to reach the jetty in the dark. The boat would be anchored some way off so it didn't get stuck in the slush closer to the jetty at low tide. While Bruno and Camille went to the guest house for the night, Baath would return to Port Blair and the Rama Raos would eat dinner at Bala's tea shop and fill the dive cylinders at 200 pounds pressure.

They filled seven cylinders. Each cylinder took fifteen minutes to fill. It took one and three quarters of an hour to fill all the cylinders. They needed six cylinders for the dives, two for each diver and one as reserve in case a cylinder sprang a leak. After the cylinders were filled they went back to the dinghy to sleep. It took three hours to reach Cinq island from Chidiyatapoo. Each dive lasted between forty-five minutes to an hour. After the dive they had to rest for an hour. If they left at seven in the morning, they usually got back by five. It was always dark by the time they reached Chidiyatapoo.

As they returned to Chidiyatapoo on the fourth night Bruno told Baath that Camille was not happy with the guest house at Chidiyatapoo. There was no warm water available for a bath. Sometimes there was no running water either. The food too was not to her liking. She was having a miserable time there. He had decided to shift back to Bay Island hotel in Port Blair. So Baath shifted all the equipment back to Wandoor, charged the tanks and asked Rama Rao to take the dinghy to Port Blair. Rama Rao took the dinghy to Pannighat where he lived, across the waters from Bay Island. They had a one day break from diving as they shifted.

After diving continuously for four or five days, it was necessary to take a day's rest before they flew out from Port Blair. The twenty four hours was a no flying time, a standard procedure recommended to divers for their well being. In that time the nitrogen that accumulated in the body during the period of diving exits the body which could otherwise cause decompression sickness, leading to paralysis, even death. There would be a drop in pressure when they flew and at the same time the nitrogen volume in their bloodstream could increase which would lead to complications starting with shortness of breath.

While diving, at every depth there are stoppages to relieve the pressure acting on the body and to let the nitrogen leave the body. In addition to the stoppages during diving Baath usually allowed safety stops as well, a compulsory stop for the safety of the divers, at five metres for three or five minutes at three metres, depending on the depth of the dive. This acts as decompression. During ascent the diver can ascend only at a certain speed, typically ten metres a minute before every stoppage. During the stoppage the nitrogen bubbles leave the body through the lungs. Uncontrolled ascent or descent causes impairment in reflexes and senses that results in temporary feeling of euphoria which can lead to anxiety attacks and delayed reaction to environment and errors of judgment that puts the diver in harm's way. In the Navy Baath was used to saturation dives. That happened when at a certain depth the body can no longer absorb any more nitrogen. Once the body is saturated with nitrogen the decompression time is set. It does not increase. Deep sea divers working in oil rigs spend days in the water in this manner, staying in diving bells or diving chambers that are pressurized at the same pressure as on the outside. There is an air lock for them to get in and out of the pressure chamber. This way divers can spend a long time underwater, come up in the diving chamber and decompress in a decompression chamber, typically for eight to ten hours before they leave.

For recreational dives, Baath restricted the depth to about thirty metres. There was no decompression chamber in Andaman and Nicobar islands. The nearest one was at Phuket, in Thailand. To get there a small aircraft flying at a certain height would have to take him in case of an emergency. Most islands in Andaman had extensive fringing reefs. Often the reef began close to the shore line, and most of the reefs were within thirty to forty metres of depth. After that the gradients usually fell steeply. Visibility decreased rapidly at those depths. There was little point in diving at those depths.

Bruno and Camille rested for a day at Bay Island hotel. Bruno suggested that for the last day of the dive they should go to some other place, to the north. They had dived enough in the south around Wandoor, off Rutland and in Cinq. After consulting the charts, Baath suggested that they could dive off Sir Hugh Rose Island. This was almost due east of Port Blair, south of both Neil Island and Havelock Island, where most tourists went. The fringing reefs there were at a depth of eighteen or twenty metres, not more. These were not big or long coral reefs. The sea bed was rocky and Baath had caught many fish there. They could see some good fish. The island was 20 nautical miles away from Port Blair. They decided to go there the next day for the dive and Baath marked the spot on the chart and told Rama Rao to prepare for the trip accordingly. Himanshu Mallik, who worked for Baath and managed the ticketing, said he'd like to come and see them off at the Bay Island jetty in the morning. He lived at the Military Engineering service quarters, where his father worked. It was a ten-minute walk to Baath's house.

The next morning when Baath woke up, everybody else was sleeping. The children didn't have school that day, even though they were in the middle of examinations. They could afford to sleep longer. Baath shook Mona awake to tell her he was going diving. Where, she asked, sleepily. Chota Neil, he said. Chota Neil was the local name for Sir Hugh Rose Island. Okay, she said sleepily, turning over. When will you be back? In the evening, Baath replied.

By the time Baath was ready to leave home, Himanshu was outside the door. From his house to Bay Island hotel, it was only ten minutes away by his motorcycle. They went to Dilanipur to pack some food for the day. The eateries had not yet opened, and all they found at that time were a few vadas, some bhajjis and samosas , which they bought. They stopped at another shop that was opening and bought a couple of bottles of mineral water, two litres each. This would be food for the Rama Raos and Baath for the day. Bay Island hotel would pack the food for Bruno and Camille.

When they reached Bay Island hotel at six thirty in the morning, Bruno and Camille were ready to leave. They went down to the jetty. The Rama Raos had loaded the equipment on the dinghy. This was the dinghy that was presented to Baath by Admiral Virender Singh. It was about 35 feet long. They had fitted two long benches, one on each side in the front. There was a bench athwart the ship where people could wear their diving equipment and roll off the dinghy into the water, backwards. Behind that was a ladder made of GI pipe. That ladder was kept inside the boat but when the divers finished the dive, the ladder would be fixed to the side so people could climb into the boat easily. It was clamped to the side of the boat. The ladder was kept behind the engines of the boat. Right behind that was a small platform for the crew to sit. There was a canvas cover in front of the dinghy for shade. There was another smaller tarpaulin that the crew used in the back for shade. Six feet by three feet. The framework for the cover was cane and wood. The cover didn't come right up to the gunwale. There was a gap of about one and a half feet. For those in the boat to see through.

Five of them were going for the dive: Rama Rao Sr, Rama Rao Jr, Bruno, Camille, and Baath. They got into the boat and were about to cast off when Himanshu said he wanted to come along too. He had never been to Sir Hugh Rose Island and he wanted to come. Baath reminded Himanshu that he hadn't told his parents. Himanshu replied that they'd be back in the late afternoon and that would be fine. It was his birthday and Baath did not want to refuse. So they set off. It was not yet seven in the morning. The sun was warm, the water was shimmering. The sea was flat and calm. As they passed the mouth of the channel that led to the harbour, the light house was some distance away, on a hillock. Below it were rocks where the waves dashed. A little to the front of it the funnel of a ship and part of the bow stuck out of the sea. The metal hull was missing in some places where it was above the water line. Bruno asked what that wreck was.

That's the Karunya Pacific, replied Baath.

The Karunya Pacific

One day a young man rang the bell at Baath's house. He introduced himself as the son of Admiral Bansal who headed the Indian Navy operations in Andaman and Nicobar Islands. He wanted to go diving with Baath. Your father is the Navy's Number One man here. Why don't you ask him? Baath responded. You can go diving with the Navy, can't you? Bansal replied that he had gone diving twice with the naval divers but it hadn't been much fun. The navy divers constantly worried about his safety and didn't give him much freedom. They didn't take him down beyond a depth of three metres.

So one Sunday, Baath and Mona organized a dive picnic. They took twelve youngsters, along with Bansal to North Bay and taught them the basics in very shallow waters. Then they were taken to deeper waters. Bansal and a girl in the group showed a natural talent for diving and Baath took them to depths of fifteen or sixteen metres off the reefs. They saw fish and corals and turtles. The water was transparent. There was not a cloud in the sky and afterwards they went for another dive. Bansal enjoyed the dive. When he dived with his father's subordinates they attached a chord to him. He was fussed over and supervised all the time. Baath set him free underwater. Bansal was so overjoyed that when he went back home he could not resist telling his father that he had gone diving with Commander Baath and had enjoyed himself immensely underwater. By comparison, he told Admiral Bansal, the naval experience had been pathetic.

The next week Admiral Bansal summoned Commander Baath to his office at the naval headquarters. The admiral came straight to the point: 'You took my son diving. Now you take me diving as well. I don't enjoy the navy diving-shiving either.'

The following Sunday Baath and Mona went to North Bay again, this time in the Admiral's yacht, Baath's dinghy trailing behind with the tanks and the equipment. The weather held and for the first dive they went to a depth of twelve metres. The admiral was comfortable wearing the buoyancy jackets that were used for recreational diving. Navy dives were a no-frills affair. The diver had to work much harder finning all the time. Buoyancy jackets made the experience so much more relaxed. A button controlled the buoyancy: the jacket could be inflated or deflated to rise or sink respectively. It was as easy as that. The first thing the admiral said when they surfaced was that he was going to procure the jackets for the navy and start a diving club so the naval people could enjoy diving. Over lunch and beer he asked whether there was a wreck around nearby where they could go diving.

Wrecks made for great dive spots but there was no wreck nearby. Once a ship sinks, reef starts forming around the wreck and the fish start living inside the wreck. Colonies start building around and over the wreck. Eels, groupers, barracudas, sharks and many other fish start living inside the ship's compartments and later the reef starts forming on the ship itself. Wrecks are divers' favourite spot.

Then the admiral said, You know, we are supposed to be sinking a ship soon.

The Karunya Pacific had been sailing from somewhere in East Asia with its holds full of cement. It was going towards Colombo when it developed engine trouble and had drifted a while before running aground on one of the islands of the Nicobar group. Ships sailing in the area generally took a short cut through the Ten Degree Channel. Once past the channel they headed further west. This ship ran aground on one of the islands there. The owners, NRIs from the Gulf area, requested that it be freed from the island. The navy sent some divers to assess the damage and did some work on the hull and when the tide was highest Coast Guard tugs and salvage vessels went there and pulled the Karunya Pacific out from the sand bar and towed it all the way to Port Blair where it remained anchored in the harbour. It came under the care of the Port Management Board. For all the efforts, the salvaging and towing, the bills had run into a huge amount. The owners could not pay up and said they didn't want the ship any longer.

There was a case in court and the Karunya Pacific was finally declared as a wreck and the Navy was given the responsibility to sink the ship in deep waters. The ship had by then been so long at the harbour they did not know what condition the hull was in. If it sprang a leak and sank in the harbour it would become a navigational hazard. The ship was about eighty metres long and could carry about 3000 tonnes of cargo. The cement was removed and sold to pay for the port charges, the berthing and the looking after. The crew was an all-foreign crew. They had been imprisoned and released after two or three years. All the Navy had to do now was to take a tug from the Port Management Board to tow the Karunya Pacific out into deep waters and sink it.

Admiral Bansal asked Baath: Why not sink the Karunya Pacific somewhere handy where it would not affect the movement of ships and where it could be sunk in waters deep enough for it to become a wreck and a dive spot? Baath responded that it would be great if that were to happen. So Admiral Bansal cancelled the towing that was scheduled and consulted the Harbour Master who said as long as it didn't sink in the path of the ships and was outside the harbour limits, he didn't mind.

Baath suggested a spot where the Karunya Pacific could be sunk, about two hundred metres away from a reef and at a depth of 40 metres of water. From that height, divers would be diving into the wreck which would be at a depth of 25 or 30 metres. Any depth shallower wouldn't be much of a dive. They visited the spot and fixed the day for the ship to be towed there and sunk.

The sea was choppy the day the tug began towing the ship out of Haddow and out of the harbour. The north easterly monsoon had set in. The tug strained through the waves and just after the ship left the harbour the tow rope snapped all of a sudden. It was a nylon rope and had a swift backlash. The end of which snaked like a missile towards the tug and hit one of the crew on the head. The force was so massive that the nylon sliced his forehead like a sharp dao slicing off the top of a coconut clean. There was still so much recoil left in the thick nylon rope that it snaked swiftly and hit another crew member in the chest, breaking a few ribs. The rest of the crew were so shocked that all they could do was stare at their headless colleague thrash about on the deck as life went out of him and the other colleague crumpled in a heap groaning with pain, holding his chest. The crew now refused to tow the Karunya Pacific which began to drift. The tug turned around and rushed back into the harbour. The naval ship in attendance sent out boats and naval divers clambered aboard the drifting ship and put out another tow to the naval ship which finally started towing the Karunya Pacific out. The naval ship began to head for the spot which had been identified, north of the North Point lighthouse. When it reached the spot it positioned the ship. It was too close to the shore for the naval ship to fire upon it and sink it. The plan was to send out divers to the ship once the permission to sink it was given and set charges below the hull and blow a hole. Once the charges were set the ship would let go of the tow line and sink.

The sea was rough when the naval ship anchored off the spot. The captain feared the tow line would break again so he ordered it to be released and then requested permission to sink the ship. In the north easterly monsoon the sea was flowing towards the shore. As soon as the tow line was free the abandoned ship began to drift towards the shore. The chief of staff, the commodore in charge of Chennai Naval headquarters sent an order to hold the operation. He said he wanted to see the ship sink and was coming in by helicopter. The Karunya Pacific kept edging towards the shore, its bow slowly turning towards the lighthouse. It was impossible to connect it with the tow rope now with the sea heaving so much. The ship hit the rocks before the charges could be set and before the helicopter turned up. From where they watched helplessly they could hear the long grinding crunch of metal on rock. The aft part of the ship now rested in about eight or nine metres of water. Even afterwards there was no sign of the helicopter with the commodore in it. There was nothing more they could do but watch the Karunya Pacific slowly sink as the seawater flooded the hull.

Over the years scrap metal dealers came stealthily in dinghies bringing blow torches and cut away the Karunya Pacific plate by plate and took it away to sell as scrap. All that was left now was the mast and the funnel which defiantly stuck out over the waves at high tide. The underwater portion of the hull was also intact. At low tide the giant rusted propeller can be seen, waiting patiently to be taken away by a more enterprising metal thief.

Lights in the Dark

It is two thirty in the morning. Rama Rao is on the watch, manning the rudder. Around him all he can see is the dark sea. Everything is still. It is difficult to make out if the dinghy is moving. The sea is gentle as it laps against the dinghy lulling everyone to sleep. Rama Rao is finding it difficult to stay awake. All the rest are asleep. Rama Rao Jr is sleeping near him, with his mouth open, snoring from time to time. Baath is fast asleep on the plank. That is the only sound that Rama Rao hears other than the sea around him. Rama Rao yawns and stretches and stands up to get rid of the tingle in his left leg from sitting still in the same position for such a long time. He feels thirsty all of a sudden but he knows that he cannot drink any more of the remaining water. He has already drunk his quota. He wonders if his wife is awake, thinking of him. He tries not to think of what could be happening at home. It is five days since he left home. He desperately tries to push the thoughts of home and his wife and daughters even as he pictures the younger one running up to him. His eyes well up with tears as he wipes them away with his hand. He can hardly see through the tears.

He sees something glisten in the horizon. He keeps wiping the tears away but the glimmer in the horizon doesn't go away.

Finally he brings his lungi to his face and wipes his eyes with it. He squints through the dark night. Yes, he can see it in the distance, a light. It seems so strange to him now that he keeps staring at it. Then Rama Rao scrambles towards Baath and shakes him awake.

Saab there is a ship, a ship!

Baath wakes up at once and sits up. He sees Rama Rao pointing to the forward side, over the bow of the dinghy. Baath stands up; he can see the light clearly. It looks like a ship, a big ship. It keeps coming steadily nearer. Baath wakes everybody up. They are all excited.

We have to start a fire to attract the ship, Baath says, and begins to give instructions. He asks Bruno to get his camera and start flashing the ship. Baath pulls his tee shirt over his head and asks Bruno for the knife to cut a portion of it. He asks Rama Rao to get the remaining part of the tyre that had been cut. Himanshu gets the lube oil. There are still enough tyres left to burn and there is plenty of lube oil left. Baath is confident they can get a good fire going. Bruno gives him the lighter from his kit and readies to flash the ship.

The ship is much nearer now. It is passing towards the stern of the dinghy. It is now about two and a half miles away. It is a big ship, all lit up. It has more than two streaming lights and sidelights. From the dinghy it looks like a floating carnival.

Bruno is flashing the ship with his camera. Baath soaks the portion of the tee shirt in the lube oil and holds a lighter to it and it begins to burn. Baath can feel the heat from the leaping flame. He waits for the tyre to catch fire. At first all it does is give out smoke. Then it begins to burn. Baath forks it with the rod they had used earlier to signal the ship they had passed in the daylight and lifts the rod waving it from side to side. If a flame or a light moved from side to side it is meant to be a distress signal.

Baath's arms are hurting from waving the rod. He calls Himanshu to help him. The flame is bright yellow and orange and they can feel the heat searing their skin and bits of burning tee shirt fall on them as they wave the tyre. The ship does not change course. It keeps sailing down the stern and moves resolutely on.

Why aren't they stopping to help us, Camille asks, her voice shrill with anxiety.

The only reason I can think is that these waters are prone to piracy, Baath says. Most masters won't stop in these waters to investigate such lights in the night. It is chancy for them. They might stop and turn back if we are able to talk to them on a radio frequency. I can't think of any other reason why that ship is ignoring us.

Do you think they are ignoring us, Himanshu asks.

If you were on that bridge and on the watch would you not have seen the light?

Himanshu keeps quiet. They watch the ship as it keeps sailing into the dark night till they can see it no more. It is almost three thirty in the morning. Pessimism hangs heavy in the air. No one wants to go back to sleep. Baath knows that for the first time in five days they are contemplating the possibility that they may not survive. Their hopes have disappeared along with the ship into the darkness that engulfs them.

Baath can almost see the question forming in Rama Rao's mind.

Don't worry, he says, by now they would have missed us and they will be looking for us. They will find us soon. We have enough water anyway.

The silence is oppressive.

Do you know where we are drifting to? he asks Himanshu.

We are going away from home sir, Himanshu says, his voice breaking. That much I know.

We are drifting to Thailand. Have you ever been to Thailand?

No sir.

Do you have a passport?

No sir.

Well, look at the bright side. We are going to Thailand and you are going there without passport. We will go there for free now. Without ticket and without passport. Don't worry at all.

Himanshu doesn't say anything. He wonders if they will ever step on land. He is thinking of his mother. Five days had passed without him having eaten a morsel.

Rama Rao is thinking of his wife and children. He wonders if his brother-in-law will look after his family when he is gone.

Baath wishes the sea was rough and the weather bad. The dinghy would have moved much faster. Now they had all the time in the world to think of their situation. As the sun comes up, silence envelopes the dinghy. Baath can no longer bear the silence. He goes up to Camille and says, It is tomorrow already.

I know, says Camille. Today is the 16th. If you add the numbers it is seven. Maybe today somebody will find us. Maybe today is our lucky day.

Seven is not my lucky number. My lucky number is eight, Baath responds.

Why is that? Asks Camille.

I was born on the 26th. They add up to eight. If we are found, maybe we will be found tomorrow. Not today.

The Search

After seventy two hours of searching for Baath and the dinghy there didn't seem any point in continuing. Established protocol was if the target could not be found within the stipulated time, seventy two hours in this case, it would be futile to continue. The search had to be abandoned. The Air Force and the Navy could not deploy so much of their assets for the sole purpose of searching for six people for such a long time. They had other commitments to meet.

DIG Dey thought otherwise. He had a gut feeling that Coast Guard would find Baath. Many years ago, when he had been posted in Mangalore, in command of the coast guard ship Vijaya, he had been in charge of a search and rescue operation of a fisherman who had gone missing. Off the Mangalore coast, fishermen fish at night. The waters are thick with fishing boats as well as merchant navy vessels that ply very close to the coast. Dey received a communication from the collectorate to look for a fisherman who had gone missing after the boat he had been fishing in was hit by a merchant navy ship. The boat had seven other fishermen who had swum four nautical miles to the shore after the fishing boat broke in the impact and sank. One fisherman did not make it to the shore. Vijaya was patrolling in the area when the message came from the collectorate. The

Coast Guard launched a search but for 24 hours they could find no trace of the fisherman. The following evening, shortly before sunset Dey launched a final helicopter sortie. The helicopter climbed to 2500 feet and after a while in the light of the setting sun saw something white on the water. When it went down to investigate it turned out to be a piece of thermocol, about three feet wide. Holding on to it was a man, his back to the sky. The helicopter radioed the location and went away. The Coast Guard ship came and picked up the fisherman who was cold and barely breathing. He was brought into the Medical Investigation Room aboard Vijaya where he subsequently recovered.

Dey was not one to give up till there was no other option. His appreciation of the situation was a little different from the other agencies. Since he was the head of the Coast Guard he was at liberty to deploy his ships and planes and he personally supervised this. Baath was a friend. Both were ex-navy and they interacted socially as well. Dey shifted the search from the east and south eastern side to the north and north eastern side. As per the prediction and the wind condition the dinghy, if the engine had broken down, may have drifted in a south easterly direction. But Baath's dinghy had been caught in a squall. A squall was not predictable. It could come from any direction and head in any direction. Moreover, it was not as if there had been only one squall in the area. Over the days and nights a series of squalls had hit the area where the dinghy had gone. DIG Dey noticed though that the direction of the subsequent squalls were generally north east. So he decided to search that area as well since the Coast Guard had already scoured the south east. In any case his aircraft had to fly every day.

Dey took it upon himself as a challenge. He personally supervised the search. Everyday a Dornier took off for a sortie in the morning and another in the evening. The evening sortie would return by sunset after which time it was too dark to search. Dey deployed Varad, an offshore patrol vessel, in the northern sector and a dornier covered the area too. He stationed himself in a small inshore patrol vessel Kanak Latha Barua. From there, he was in direct communication with the aircraft and the other assets which had been deployed into the sea to search for Baath and his companions. Each sortie lasted four or five hours over the search area. After every sortie the plane would report back to Dey with the search results. He would then shift the search to another area.

It was difficult looking for a small dinghy from the sky. Many factors came into play, the angle of sight, visibility, the height at which the aircraft was flying, sea conditions. From the air the search target, the dinghy, was very small and if the waves were high it could very easily merge with the waves. Every day Dey called Mona and gave her a briefing on what the Coast Guard had done during the day in its continuing search for Baath.

Everyday Mona could hear the planes take off to look for her husband. The phone calls she attended seemed endless. On the second day she imagined they must be really starving wherever they were, Baath and those with him, unless they were on an island. She knew Baath and Rama Rao were hardy survivors. She didn't know Himanshu all that well. Mona felt sad for Camille. She knew whatever was happening out there must be terrible for Camille. Mona was also worried that they might've fallen into the hands of pirates or gunrunners.

Gunrunning was common between Thailand to Myanmar via the remote islands of the Andaman and Nicobar. Once there was an incident when gunrunners had rounded up dozens of Thai fishermen and anchored off Narcodam Island before they were caught by Indian navy and army. Six of them had been shot dead, and once the coast guard had to fire on poachers who wouldn't surrender. Poachers carried sharp knives or daos, with which they were handy. Mona hoped Baath wouldn't run into poachers who frequented the islands for shark fins, sea cucumber and take away timber after felling trees in the uninhabited islands.

On the third day Himanshu's father came to visit Mona. Himanshu was his only son, and he looked sad and on the point of tears. He didn't talk much. He was the picture of helplessness. What do we do, madam? he asked.

Don't worry they will be back. Himanshu will be back. It might take twenty days for all we know, but they will be back. Don't worry.

He began to look even more worried at the prospect of not seeing his son for another seventeen days.

On the fifth day, Himanshu's father came in bent and low. He looked distraught. He came in and sat without speaking. Mona had to prompt him.

Madam, I do not know how to tell this... how to ask, Himanshu's father began tentatively.

What is it? Tell me, Mona said, encouragingly.

Madam I am told there is a baba to whom you have to give rice and dhoop and he can tell us where they are… Himanshu's father's voice trailed off.

We have to do everything we can, Mona said. Whatever you want to do, do it. I will get you whatever you want and we will do whatever that has to be done to find your son and my husband.

When he left, Himanshu's father walked a little straighter. He looked more hopeful. Nothing came out of it, though.

Just the previous day Rama Rao's people had trooped in. A seer had given them the divination that Rama Rao was on Cinq Island. Some thought they should approach the Karen, who were experts on sea currents around the islands, to determine where they could be.

Mona explained to them that during storms currents were difficult to predict.

The Karens know, madam, they said diffidently.

How can you be so sure?

They have special powers madam.

The next time a friend from the Navy came home Mona asked: Supposing, just supposing, they are in or around Cinq?

The navy sent divers to Cinq, where there was not a soul.

With so many people coming and going and all the calls she was attending there was no way Mona could keep the information that Baath had gone missing from her sons.

Baba has not come back, and his boat is probably drifting, and they may have run out of fuel, Mona told her sons.

When will baba be back, they asked. The children didn't sound anxious. Karan and Aman thought their father was having an adventure. Nishant was too young to comprehend the situation.

Their teachers at school kept asking them, Any news of your papa?

Baba has gone diving but he has not come back. Something has happened but he will come back, they told the teachers.

The teachers called Mona to say, Your boys are so brave.

Mona tried to be strong but there were times when she felt really low. It happened when Dey called her up and abruptly said, Mona, we found a wreck…

There was a heavy silence at the other end while Mona waited for Dey to complete the sentence.

You will have to come and identify it. She had to sit down when she heard it. For the first time, Mona was scared.

We found pieces. Pieces of the dinghy, Dey continued, You have to come and identify if it is the same dinghy...

What colour? Mona found herself asking after a while, What colour is the wreck?

Red and white. There is thermocol stuck on the inside of the wood, Dey said.

Mona was relieved. There was no red and white on Baath's dinghy. There was no thermocol either.

That is not the one, Mona asserted. It can't be the one...

You will still have to come and see it, Dey insisted.

But Mona didn't want to go. She could not do it. Mona sent Goriah, the one person who knew the dinghy almost as much as Rama Rao Sr and he came back smiling to say that it was not the one and it was part of a trawler not a dinghy.

The second time was even worse. Some friends dropped in and one of them said, during the course of conversation, Hope they haven't come across Burmese poachers...

Poachers were something to worry about because they were as unscrupulous as they were desperate. They would do anything not to get caught. They were very handy with long, curving daos. Local fishermen were terrified of Burmese poachers and their murderous daos and left them alone whenever they chanced upon them, either at sea or in one of the uninhabited islands. Mona began to think of the diving equipment in the dinghy and the cameras and Camille. For poachers all this would be tempting. Rama Rao could probably fight Mona reasoned, although he was so diminutive. Baath had no experience with daos. Bruno and Camille could do nothing to save themselves. Burmese poaching expeditions had sometimes seven or eight people. They would have outnumbered Baath and his crew. Thinking of this, Mona felt depressed.

Mona resisted telling Baath's relatives that he was missing. Her friends kept insisting that this had to be done. Mona had told her parents and sister that Baath was missing but she didn't want to call Baath's mother or brother. It seemed to her to be some kind of final act, that if she made that call it would be as if Baath would never come back, and that was unthinkable. Mona's friends kept insisting that Baath's mother had a right to know that her son was missing. You cannot not tell them, a friend persisted.

Finally, Mona called up her brother-in-law and told him the story sketchily and kept telling him not to worry and not to tell her mother-in-law. Baath will be back, she kept telling her brother-in-law. It will take fifteen or twenty days but he will be back.

Everything is fine, she told him. We are all fine. We are waiting for him to come back. He will come back. I will let you know when he comes back. Mona's brother-in-law told his mother. When Mona's mother–in-law called, over the phone Mona sensed a helplessness and sadness far more than she was experiencing. Her brother-in-law came on the line and kept repeating that he was coming over immediately. Mona kept telling him not to. She didn't want that. There was too much for her to deal with already.

The only time Mona was alone was at night after the children had gone to sleep. That was the time she was alone with her thoughts. After everybody had gone and the lights were out. That was when she felt utterly alone and helpless.

Off Sir Hugh Rose Island

Beyond where the waves washed over the ruined hulk of the Karunya Pacific, stood the North Bay Lighthouse, which overlooked the stretch of sea across Ross Island. Once the dinghy crossed the lighthouse it was the open sea, all the way to Sir Hugh Rose. From the dinghy they couldn't see either Neil Island or Chota Neil, as Sir Hugh Rose was called. The sea glistened with the sun over their heads. After a while they ate their breakfast. The hotel had packed sandwiches, boiled eggs, and a few fruits for Bruno and Camille. They ate sitting in the front, talking to each other in low voices. Baath joined the others in the back and shared some of the food they had bought from Dilanipur, saving some for lunch.

When we go back this evening, we can have a drink to celebrate your birthday, Baath told Himanshu. *Kya piyoge?* Teachers whiskey?

Kuch bhi chalega saab, Himanshu responded.

When they reached the vicinity of Sir Hugh Rose Island it was ten in the morning and hot. Everybody kept drinking water. It took some time to find a suitable spot for diving. The depth had to be right and the spot nice. They had a depth finder but no GPS. Baath had loaned it to a friend who had formed a Reef Watch association and who had gone off to mark the reefs off Nicobar Island south of Port Blair, some three or four days ago, taking the GPS. Baath had marked the spot on the chart and tried to determine by observing the various features of Sir Hugh Rose if they were in the correct spot, directing the dinghy all the while till he was sure. Around ten thirty, Baath pronounced himself satisfied that this was the spot he had marked on the map. It was a mile off Sir Hugh Rose.

That is when Baath, Bruno and Camille entered the water for the first dive. They planned to do two dives, each lasting about an hour. They didn't carry any lights for night diving because they didn't plan to dive in the night. If everything went according to plan they would be back in Port Blair at five or five thirty and wrap up the evening over a couple of drinks to celebrate Himanshu's birthday. The next day Camille and Bruno planned to visit the tourist spots in and around Port Blair while they waited for the nitrogen to exit their bodies before they flew off.

When they entered the water, the sea was absolutely calm and like an endless liquid mirror. Usually Baath would tell the dinghy master what route the divers would follow while they were underwater. If there was no current they would surface closer to the boat after the dive, navigating underwater with a compass. If there was a strong current Baath would indicate where they would surface and the dinghy would meet the divers at the designated spot. As the divers drifted underwater the boat drifted on the surface, almost maintaining the same rate of drift. If there was a current a diver would know as soon as he entered the water.

That day there was hardly any current. The divers went down twenty metres. The light was good. The dive site had large isolated rocks, sea fans spreading on top of some of them.

Blue, beige, red, white fans stood like silent sentinels. Baath saw a big fan, spreading ten feet tall and five feet wide and beckoned to Bruno who took pictures of hundreds of yellow and blue fish swimming past them. They saw emperor fish swimming among the rocks, and some sea anemone.

Bruno was photographing a purple anemone which was swimming along when he found the light wavering. From the middle distance, a giant grouper began swimming towards them. They saw the cleaner fish before they saw the grouper. It looked as though the behemoth was enveloped in a yellow and black cloud, as it swam majestically, ignoring the commotion of a hundred cleaner fish swimming along with it, picking on the barnacles growing on its head like a crown. It must have been at least two hundred kilos, its giant mouth curving in a thick lipped grimace. Baath indicated to the others that they should sit down on the sea bed and watch the grouper go, without attracting its attention. A grouper swallowed its prey whole by going near a fish opening its giant mouth and sucking the water along with the fish inside its mouth. Groupers ate everything. They were the first to take bait, even if it was another grouper. As the giant grouper swam inexorably nearer, they crouched on the sea bed, Baath wishing he had a spear gun but knowing that it wouldn't help. Some months ago he had come close to a group of three big groupers swimming one after another in a line. At that time he had carried a spear gun with him. Impulsively, he had shot at the last grouper with the spear gun. The spear hit the grouper behind the gills and fell to the sea bed. The big grouper had swum on imperviously. But now this giant grouper looked as though it was intent on converging on them. As they shrank away from its path the grouper swam on into the gathering darkness.

It was getting darker and then brighter as the light fluctuated. From twenty metres deep in the water they couldn't see the surface. Baath thought maybe there were clouds forming in the sky. Even so visibility was less than fifteen metres. They had been underwater for an hour and ten minutes. Both Bruno and Camille indicated they were happy with the dive and they surfaced, close to the dinghy. Clouds had formed in the sky and the sea water rippled.

When they came aboard the dinghy, Rama Rao mentioned that it had been raining while they were diving.

They had to wait about an hour before they could dive again. They started to eat as it began to rain again. The wind picked up. While they waited the weather turned nasty gradually. The wind came gusting and cold and it looked as though it was going to squall. A squall usually lasted for about fifteen to twenty minutes and once it passed things usually got better. Baath thought if they waited the squall out they could still go for a second dive. So they waited. Soon it stopped raining but the wind didn't let up. The wind whipped up the waves and the sea became choppy. At around one they decided that it was not worth diving anymore that day off Sir Hugh Rose. Visibility was dropping and the waves had begun to come on big. They had to get back to Port Blair and they could make out that the sea was against them. That would slow them down. If the weather improved by the time they reached Port Blair and if the visibility was better perhaps they could dive around North Bay. Rama Rao heaved up the anchor and they headed for Port Blair. Baath told Rama Rao to keep Sir Hugh Rose behind him and take a bearing west for Port Blair. They would find themselves north of Port Blair in about three and a half or four hours. All they had to do then was go along the coast and enter the harbour. There wasn't much light now and the sky was overcast. Dark clouds were steadily gathering. It was raining as well. Visibility was down to less than a mile, and they could not make out the shape of Sir Hugh Rose Island any longer. Sometime later it stopped raining but darker clouds began to loom up from the port bow side. Baath thought it could be some pre-monsoon activity. Monsoon came in May, still less than a couple of months away.

An hour and a half later a drizzle began. The squall had sharpened the wave tops and they were breaking and foaming. Now the wind had died down a bit but the waves came on smooth and big. The dinghy bobbed in the waves. Rama Rao Jr who had been chewing sukka all this while turned towards the sea to spit it out. That was when, squinting through the thin drizzle, the whales caught Rama Rao's eye.

The Plane

On the morning of March 17, the Coast Guard Dornier searches along the International Boundary line. In the first three hours it locates a naval ship, three Myanmarese trawlers, two Indonesian boats and one merchant ship, M V Santhosh.

* * *

Baath swims up to Camille and tells her: Today is the seventeenth.

I know, I'm counting the days.

It is my lucky day.

So you told me.

We will get picked up today.

I believe you.

No. Really. I believe we will get picked up today.

I believe you.

Camille looks at the sky. There is not a cloud up there.

How far away do you think we are from Thailand? she asks Baath.

So you don't believe me?

I believe you. I just want to know how far away we are from Thailand.

Baath doesn't answer. There is one full cylinder of water left and there are two litres of water in another cylinder. The air is still. The dinghy is moving very little with the sea.

What if we get picked up today? Baath asks Camille.

What about it?

What will you give up if we get picked up today?

Camille squints up at the sky as though to convey the impression that she is thinking about it.

Come on. It can't be all that tough. There must be something that must be worth sacrificing in order to be rescued today.

You guarantee it?

It is my lucky day! What better guarantee can there be?

You are really optimistic about this, aren't you?

You are not telling me what you will give up.

I have to think about it.

Well hurry up. You haven't got all day.

Camille is laughing now.

Ok. I will give up smoking, she says finally.

Say that again?

I won't smoke any more if we are rescued today.

Sure?

Sure.

If you get picked up today, what is the first thing you would like to have? Would you like a cigarette?

No. I would like a big glass of coke with lots of ice in it!

Not a cigarette?

Never again a cigarette if I am rescued today. I will go for coke, with ice, a tall glass of coke with lots of ice. With big drops of water condensing around the glass and running into my hands. What would you like?

Cold beer. A bottle of chilled beer.

Well, today is our lucky day then. You will have cold beer and I will have coke with ice.

Right. But I am also going to smoke a cigarette.

Ok. I will watch you smoke the cigarette.

You promise not to inhale second hand smoke when I do that?

I will hold my breath.

I can't wait for that beer then.

In his diving watch, Baath sees the time. It is 12.34. Half his lucky day is gone.

* * *

At exactly one forty two in the afternoon Baath hears a small droning sound. It is not the sound of a jet. He looks around to see if anybody else has heard it. Nobody seems to have heard it. He begins to think maybe his ears are playing tricks on his mind. He asks Himanshu who is clinging on to the rope next to him.

Kuch sunayi de raha hai? Can you hear anything?

Kuch nahin sunayi de raha hai, Himanshu responds. I can't hear anything.

Baath can hear it again. It sounds like a turboprop engine.

Hawai jahaj ki awaaz aa rahi hai, he tells Himanshu. There is a plane coming.

Woh to har roz sunayi deta hai sahib, Himanshu says. We hear that everyday sir. He is referring to the jets that flew overheard.

No listen carefully, I can hear a turboprop plane, not a jet plane.

I can't hear anything, says Himanshu.

Dhyan se suno, sunayi dega. Listen carefully, you can hear it.

Himanshu listens intently for a while and then says, I still can't hear anything. *Mujhe nahin sunayi de raha hai*. I can't hear anything.

Baath asks others if they could hear it. None of the others could hear a plane. Baath asks them to get into the dinghy.

Get your flash ready, he tells Bruno and clambers aboard the dinghy. As he climbs aboard he reaches out to help pull in the others one by one. Rama Rao comes up and begins to help the others into the dinghy. As he pulls in Rama Rao Jr, he lets out a shout.

Kala naag!

He points to the sea. There!

There was a black sea snake swimming around the boat right where they had been in the water clinging to the ropes. Baath estimates it to be two and a half feet long. It is the black cobra of the sea, more poisonous than the cobra on the land and more poisonous than the banded sea snake.

Camille sits down suddenly on the bench and smiles weakly at Baath and says, Well, I believe you now. Your luck has rubbed off on all of us. Chances are it could have bitten any one of us.

I told you it is my lucky day. When I get lucky I really get lucky.

Bruno is taking pictures of the snake which is swimming around the boat, just below the surface, zigzagging along, sunlight playing on its slender body.

Baath tells Bruno to get his flash ready.

Everybody can hear the drone of the plane now and all are looking up at the sky.

It is a turboprop aircraft, says Baath, maybe a Dornier or an AN 32 or something like that. Maybe they are searching for us.

We have to get the aircraft over us. We have to somehow attract its attention. Bruno, flash your camera now!

There are tyres which they could try to burn. But to make a fire would take a long time. In the sunlight a flash would be seen from much farther away.

Bruno flashes his camera at the direction of the sound, which is now distinct.

Please flash again, Baath says.

It takes more than a minute and a half for Bruno to recharge the camera now. The battery is very weak and dying.

* * *

From the air, at 3,000 feet above sea level, after about four hours of flying, Squadron Commander VK Awasthi, takes out the lunch his wife has packed. As soon as the lunchbox is opened the aroma of phulka and matar paneer envelopes the tiny cockpit. Awasthi's wife usually packed enough for everybody on board. The plane is on auto pilot as they share the lunch. Walia, the pilot, says after the first bite: If you keep giving me this kind of food I will fly the Dornier any number of days.

Awasthi smiles. After lunch Walia looks out through the cockpit glass. There are broken clouds on the horizon as well as over the sea. Then he sees a tiny flash like that of a strobe light. He is sure he saw it.

Walia turns to his co-pilot and asks, Chopra, did you see that?

No sir, I did not see anything, Chopra replies.

I am sure I saw something, Walia says.

Walia sees a light flash again.

There, did you see it now? he asks Chopra.

No, Chopra says looking in the direction Walia is looking.

I am dead sure I saw something. There is something there.

OK. Let's take the plane there to find out, instructs the Squadron Commander, watching the radar.

The Dornier changes direction. Immediately afterwards the Squadron Commander says, There is some contact, some small contact.

Then they see the dinghy. It had to be the missing dinghy they had been looking for, Baath's dinghy. It is unlikely that some other dinghy had ventured out so far.

Walia takes over the autopilot and turns it into manual mode, reduces the Dornier's speed to about one hundred and thirty five knots, puts down all the flaps, increases the rate of descent and turns around in a reciprocal heading so as not to miss the dinghy, even though it is there in the radar as well.

From the dinghy they can see the plane coming towards them again. It is a Dornier.

The aircraft is now nearly flying over the dinghy. The pilot can see it is identical to the shape and size of the missing dinghy they have been searching for the last five days.

Deputy Commandant H S Walia immediately manoeuvres the Dornier for a low pass over the dinghy at a height of about fifty metres. The dinghy is on the left as the plane passes. They are all waving.

From the dinghy Himanshu sees the plane turning around rapidly, lose height and come directly towards the dinghy. The plane is now so low that it seems to skim over the waves. Himanshu thinks it is going to hit the dinghy. The roar of the plane is now deafening and the plane passes and comes back again.

On the second pass Walia speaks into the loudhailer, 'This is the Coast Guard and we are here with you and circling around you. There is a ship nearby that'll come and fetch you. Don't worry.' The dinghy's position is now noted in the GPS. The Dornier climbs to a safe altitude of 1000 feet, contacts the Coast Guard Headquarters at Port Blair to inform them they've found the dinghy. The Dornier requests merchant navy ship MV Santhosh to change course to the dinghy and asks Coast Guard ship Vivek to do the same. Vivek diverts course towards the point of contact. It is about thirty nautical miles away, it had a helicopter on board but it would be dark soon and helicopters had the disadvantage of not being able to fly over sea in the dark. Vivek requests the Dornier to shepherd the helicopter. Which meant it had to fly over the helicopter which had no radar, so it didn't get lost over sea. MV Santhosh is informed Vivek is heading towards the dinghy so it diverts course again.

In the dinghy, Baath looks at Himanshu and says, *Dekho is baar Thailand nahin dekh paya*. I'm afraid there is no Thailand for you this time.

Himanshu begins to cry.

Camille begins to cry too and Bruno Beauregard puts his arms around her. She makes no attempt to resist. Rama Rao too has tears in his eyes. Rama Rao Jr is too stunned to say anything. He sits down silently.

Bruno begins to photograph the plane like a little boy who has seen a plane for the very first time. Baath looks for the sea snake but there is no sign of it now.

On board Vivek, Captain Prasad the master of the ship orders full speed of twenty knots per hour as he directs his ship towards the dinghy.

Anybody wants water? You can drink all you want, Baath says. But nobody wants any water now. Each of them is lost in thought.

It is a little past four in the afternoon. Vivek launches the helicopter to get the survivors onto the ship before it gets dark. The sky has turned a bright orange and the clouds look like cotton candy. The sun has begun to set.

Shortly before four thirty in the afternoon they hear the helicopter. The helicopter is now visible. It is flying low and coming towards the dinghy. When it reaches the dinghy it positions itself directly above the dinghy and descends a little. They can feel the draft from the rotors as a wide circular patch forms all around the dinghy in the sea. An air crew diver comes down on the winch onto the dinghy and hands over water and biscuits. He greets Commander Baath and says that Camille would be winched up first, then Bruno and then Baath. The helicopter could winch up only three at a time. The rest would have to stay behind for the next trip. The helicopter would take them to Vivek and come back for the rest.

Camille doesn't want to wear the winch harness. She is scared. She doesn't want to get winched up into the helicopter which is whirling overhead. The dinghy has begun to bob up and down in the backdraft from the helicopter.

Camille looks bedraggled in her short skirt and bikini. The skirt is worn to the point of fraying in patches. Her skin is a blotchy red with the sun and she looks really tired now all of a sudden. Baath and Bruno force Camille into the harness as the diver positions the harness. Camille begins to scream as she is winched up rapidly to the side of the helicopter where she is pulled in. Bruno is taking photographs.

Then it is Bruno's turn to get yanked up. He goes without a fuss. Then Baath is winched to the helicopter. There is place in the helicopter only for three people. Baath has to sit on the platform, his legs dangling outside in the air as the helicopter swings into the air and heads towards Vivek. Baaath watches the dinghy becoming smaller and smaller till it looks like a pencil and then he can see it no more in the light of the setting sun. After a while in the distance he can see the lights of the ship. Baath goes limp as a profound tiredness takes possession of him. All he wants now is a cigarette and a bottle of cold beer.

Epilogue

The commanding officer of Vivek, Commandant Prasad, was there on the deck when the helicopter landed. Prasad was an old friend of Baath. Both had served together when they had been posted in Okha in 1984. They had lived in the same bungalow. Baath had occupied a portion of it while Prasad and his wife occupied the other part. There was a stretcher on standby when the copter landed but Baath could walk and he was the first to get off. He walked straight into the outstretched arms of Prasad who hugged him tight and said, You are lucky that we found you at all. We had almost given you up.

How far are we from Thailand? Baath asked.

You are over 120 Nautical miles off Port Blair, said Prasad, giving him the position where the dinghy had been discovered. Baath calculated that they were about halfway to Myanmar, not Thailand. If the weather had continued to remain the way it was they would not have made it there either.

It is my lucky day, Baath said to Prasad.

Camille couldn't stand and was nearly blacking out. She had to be taken in a stretcher straight to the MI room where she was given a drip. Bruno was all right. He acted as though nothing had happened. He was taken to the ward room. Baath went to Prasad's room wearing his swimming trunks and what little was left of his tee shirt.

Baath was worried about the diving equipment and the dinghy. He wanted the dinghy back. Prasad said he had already messaged Port Blair that his ship would dock by eight in the morning. In the meanwhile Vivek would rendezvous with the dinghy. Prasad told Baath not to worry. Two men had already gone in the helicopter to man the dinghy.

The helicopter went back to fetch the Rama Raos and Himanshu. The air crew member who came down the winch to stay with the dinghy bought lemon juice, glucose water, water, biscuits and some bread. Rama Rao wanted a beedie but the sailor did not have any. They eagerly drank the liquids. Another sailor joined the man already in the helicopter. He had signal flares with him and communication set. Himanshu and the Rama Rama Raos were winched up to the helicopter one by one. This was the first time Rama Rao Sr had gone up in a helicopter and he was frightened as the belt was strapped on and he was harnessed to the winch. It was already dark as he sat tight on the helicopter not moving at all because the helicopter was open on both sides. He thought he could see the shape of an island ten minutes after the helicopter had been flying towards the ship but in the dark could not make out which one it was. Things looked different from the air.

In less than half an hour the helicopter was back with the Rama Raos and Himanshu. They were taken directly to the canteen. The senior Rama Rao kept asking for a beedie. There was no beedie, however, for Rama Rao. One of the officers gave him a couple of Gold Flake cigarettes. Rama Rao smoked one, dragging the smoke deep into his lungs. He had not smoked anything for a week; he relished each drag even though the cigarette was lighter than the beedies he was used to. They sat in the canteen sipping hot tea and eating pakodas. It was strange to eat after so many days of not eating.

All of them were able to bathe in the ship. Bruno and Camille were given an officer's cabin to freshen up. Baath was given a bunk in the engineer's cabin. For the first time Baath looked at himself in the mirror. He could hardly recognize himself. He looked much thinner and at least five shades darker. His beard had grown scraggly, and his eyes had sunk into his skull. His skin was flaky. The engineer had given him a pair of shorts which he wore after the bath, even though it was a little tight for him. He had also given a tee shirt which too was a little tight for him. The captain invited Baath, Bruno and Camille to join him for dinner in the master's cabin.

Baath was talking with some officers whom he knew in the officer's mess room when Camille emerged from the cabin wearing a white sailor's overhaul somebody had given her. She looked refreshed. In the clean white pressed overhaul, although it hung a little loose on her, Baath thought she was looking different, quite good. There was a big glass of coke with lots of ice waiting for her. Baath had requested for it. She smiled as she sipped her coke. Bruno was also wearing shorts and a tee shirt that had been given to him. From his pocket Baath fished out a packet of cigarettes that he had asked for earlier, and offered a cigarette to her, taking it half out of the packet, till it pointed at her.

Sure you are not going to smoke, he asked, teasingly.

Of course I am going to smoke, Camille said, laughing. She snatched the cigarette that was half out of the packet. Baath lit it for her and lit one for himself too.

After a while they came out and stood on the deck. The ship

kept sailing towards the dinghy. Baath also came out to the deck to find the Rama Raos transformed, bathed and freshened. Shortly afterwards they could see the dinghy in the distance, even though it was dark. The sailors were setting off the flares which lit up the sea around the dinghy and it was strange watching the dinghy in which they had spent six days without food. When they reached the dinghy the sailors came back on board and with a long tow rope began to tow the dinghy towards Port Blair.

Dinner at the captain's table was light and continental. Baath could hardly eat. Bruno and Camille couldn't eat much either. But Baath had his glass of cold beer then. He cupped the glass with both his hands and sipped it slowly. He discovered he could not finish even a glass. Dinner for Himanshu and the Rama Raos was rice, dal, vegetable and fish. Himanshu couldn't eat either. All he did was drink water.

After dinner the dinghy was handed over to Laxmi Bai which rendezvouzed with Vivek. Diesel was filled in the fuel tank of the dinghy and both the Rama Raos went back to the dinghy, accompanied by six sailors and food supply. Rama Rao Sr wanted beedies as well. Two packets of beedies materialised from somewhere and were given to him. The ship's crew which came onboard had wireless as well as a compass. Rama Rao asked where they had reached. Over a hundred and twenty nautical miles east of Port Blair, he was told. While Laxmi Bai kept the dinghy company, Vivek drew away and proceeded at full speed towards Port Blair. In the morning, Laxmi Bai's crew gave those in the dinghy food packets and a long tow rope and began towing the dinghy towards Port Blair. A little before nine in the morning, Rama Rao Sr spotted Chota Neil. More than an hour and a half later they entered Port Blair harbor. At the entrance the Coast Guard ship disengaged. It was eleven when the Rama Raos set foot on firm ground. Both cried with relief.

Vivek had reached Chatham jetty two and a half hours earlier. Never had Baath seen so many people swarming that jetty. As the ship cut its engine and manoeuvred to the quayside, Baath could see Mona in a white churidar dress waving at him. He felt tears surging within him. Standing on the deck Himanshu spotted his father among the crowd of people. Himanshu could see his father had begun to cry. From the deck he could see the tears streaming down his father's face, his shoulders convulsing. He had not stopped crying even when he came on board ten minutes later. The crowd surged towards the ship, rushing across the gangway. Himanshu could see his father scrambling towards him. He wanted to move towards his father but he found his legs were wobbly, and he couldn't move. When his father reached him, Himanshu had recovered enough to bend down and touch his father's feet. They hugged and he said nothing. He was still crying. In the blur of the faces and the excited voices around him all Himanshu could see was his father's tears. Don't cry Baba, I am here now, he kept saying.

For days afterwards Himanshu Mallik kept dreaming he was in the dinghy again, eating barnacles. He always told himself from then on: *Khane ke liye math jeeyo, jeene ke liye khao.* Do not live to eat, eat to live instead.

Mona saw Baath standing on the deck and waving to her. When she came on board, all Baath kept saying was, It is all because of Bruno Beauregard that this happened. It is all *his* fault.

Mona hugged Baath. He looked so thin. He could barely walk. It is all his fault, Baath was saying, again. Mona had no idea what he was talking about.

Afterword

Commander Baath now sails as a master in inter-island passenger ferries. He has started a dive center, Infinity Scuba, as well as a game fishing venture, Tightlines. He is also building a resort at Chidiyatapoo. It is near the forest guest house where Bruno and Camille briefly stayed. It is named Wild Grass. Mona helps out in these ventures.

Karan, their eldest son, is a dive instructor and looks after the diving activities of Infinity Scuba. Aman, still in school, is a trained rescue diver, as is Mona. Nishant, in middle school, is already a certified open water diver.

Himanshu continues to work with Commander Baath. He helped out with the diving operations but stopped after his eardrum perforated during a dive and ended his diving career. He now manages Tightlines. He is in charge of a small, white thirty-foot fiberglass boat that has a blue line running below the gunwale. It can seat four or five people comfortably. It has a twenty five horse power engine, a small canopy for the steering post. Himanshu and a helper take customers out game fishing. After many years looking for a bride, Himanshu has not yet found someone to marry. His parents insist he should find a girl from Kolkata. Girls his parents find for him and the ones he likes don't want to move to the Andaman and Nicobar Islands. He stays at Chidiyatapoo, where the game fishing boat is stationed.

Rama Rao Sr worked for Baath for a while after the ill-fated trip to Sir Hugh Rose Island. Then he left for Havelock Island to work for a different dive operator, taking customers out for dives as the dinghy master. He stayed in Havelock for five years after which he came back to work again for Commander Baath. He left, again, citing health reasons, and has gone back home to Panighat. He lives with his family and goes fishing in other people's boats, as part of the crew.

Rama Rao Jr stopped working with Commander Baath soon after the events of the week. He went back to live with his mother in Panighat for some years. He still goes fishing for a living. It is the only thing he knows – his father had died due to excessive drinking when he had been a boy, and one by one his three sisters found spouses and left home. Rama Rao Jr is now 36 years old and has moved back to Phoenix Bay, where he was born. He subsequently married and has two children, a boy who is five years old and another who is two. One of his sisters moved back with him, his mother, and his family after her husband abandoned her when he found another woman to live with. Rama Rao Jr still chews sukka.

Bruno Beauregard and Camille Pascal went back to the Bay Island hotel from the Coast Guard ship Vivek. Later that afternoon they were supposed to come back for a photo shoot with the Coast Guard at the Coast Guard hanger at Veer Savarkar Airport where the dorniers which searched for them were parked. Camille did not turn up. She took the first flight out of Port Blair the next day and continued onwards to France. Nothing more has been heard from her, except unconfirmed rumours that she was so traumatized by the experience that she required counselling for more than a year afterwards.

The evening after their rescue, Bruno Beauregard came to Commander Baath's house for dinner and after a few drinks got sentimental and said, 'We will always be like brothers now.' That was the last Commander Baath saw or heard of him.

